A Brief Guide to Ministry with LGBTQIA Youth

Updated Edition

Praise for the New Edition

"This guide is essential reading for anyone who works with young people and seeks to approach questions of gender and sexuality from a place of wisdom and care, especially in ministering with LGBTQIA youth. With a warm, narrative voice, Cody Sanders weaves compelling real-world case studies, important research and statistics, local and national resources, and practical guidance. I have used the previous edition of this work in undergraduate and graduate classrooms, as well as in church and community settings. This updated edition speaks directly to our current tumultuous political moment and offers vital new insights into the intersections of gender, sexuality, and neurodiversity. Whether readers are new to these conversations or deeply experienced, they will encounter a thoughtful introduction to LGBTQIA terminology and resources alongside the best practices for care and mentorship."

—Keith A. Menhinick, Lecturer in Religious Studies, Affiliate Faculty in Women's, Gender, and Sexuality Studies, Georgia State University

"As an active youth minister at a progressive church, I found the updated edition of Cody Sanders's *A Brief Guide to Ministry with LGBTQIA Youth* to be both pastorally grounded and deeply practical. Sanders weaves thoughtful theology with real-world ministry wisdom, helping leaders create spaces where LGBTQIA young people are seen, safe, and valued. I wholeheartedly recommend this guide to any church and youth ministry, especially those committed to justice, compassion, and the flourishing of every young person."

—Chris Cherry, Associate Pastor of Youth and Families, First Baptist Greensboro, North Carolina

"With characteristic clarity and authority, Cody Sanders offers this updated edition of his *Brief Guide to Ministry with LGBTQIA Youth*. Sanders argues cogently that it is more important than ever to practice LGBTQIA-affirming pastoral ministries. He patiently explains the evolving terminology related to sexuality and gender identity and invites pastors, parents, and caring adults to aim for flexibility and gender-expansive understanding. This book offers sensitive theological wisdom and potentially lifesaving practical resources; it should be on pastoral care course syllabi and on all our bookshelves."

—Mary Clark Moschella, Yale University School of Theology

"The world needs this book. It is thoughtful and informative and expertly explores the nuance of faith, humanity, identity, and the current political climate. Sanders has updated the original to reflect the ever-expanding landscape of the LGBTQIA community and the importance of allyship in today's world. This book will (once again) be an invaluable, lifesaving resource."

—Pepa Paniagua, Coordinator for Innovation
and New Ministry Development, Grace Presbytery

"Informative, vast, and practical, Sanders's work is so necessary for our world right now. This is a tremendous resource for ministry staff and laypersons seeking to better understand and support some of our most vulnerable young people—whether you're part of a faith community that is already fully open and affirming or whether you're an ally trying to provide a safe space in one that isn't there just yet."

—Becky Schroeder, Youth Minister,
Middletown Christian Church, Louisville, Kentucky

"This updated version addresses the changes and new concerns that our LGBTQIA young people are facing and responds to the very real and recent threats that have been placed on our young people in this country. As a youth pastor, I thank God for this work and for Cody Sanders's commitment to continuing the conversation so that our communities of faith are more welcoming and loving toward all God's children, especially the LGBTQIA ones."

—Shelley C. Donaldson, Associate Pastor for Youth and Mission,
First Presbyterian Church of Stamford, Connecticut

Praise for the First Edition

"Cody Sanders has condensed a lifetime of personal searching, faith, and scholarship into this remarkable book. *A Brief Guide to Ministry with LGBTQIA Youth* offers ministers and youth leaders the language, skills, and, most important, genuine encouragement needed to enter into healing pastoral conversations with LGBTQIA young people and their families and congregations. Every page matters. My students will be seeing this book on required reading lists for years to come."

—Robert C. Dykstra, Charlotte W. Newcombe Professor
of Pastoral Theology, Princeton Theological Seminary

"*A Brief Guide to Ministry with LGBTQIA Youth* is exactly that—a professional and compassionate guide that should be required reading for anyone in ministry today. With up-to-date and thorough information personalized by poignant stories, Sanders offers a window into the experience of LGBTQIA youth that is both spiritually and psychologically enlightening. This is a must-read guide that should have a prominent place in your library for frequent use."

—G. Penny Nixon, Senior Minister,
Congregational Church of San Mateo, California

"Sanders invites youth workers into the 'sacred calling' of walking alongside LGBTQIA youth who have blessed us by trusting us with their stories and struggles, providing us with the language, information, and sensitivities we need to share and embody God's love for them where they are, just as they are. A must-read for any adult committed to honoring the lives and dignity of young people."

—Elizabeth W. Corrie, Associate Professor
in the Practice of Youth Education and Peacebuilding,
Director of the Youth Theological Initiative,
Candler School of Theology, Emory University

"Sanders has done a great job in identifying and articulating the fluidity in language with reference to gender, gender identity, and sexual orientation. His glossary alone is an invaluable tool as clergy and layfolk alike navigate the identities and gender queerness of our emerging world. He also provides much insight, highlighting the challenges and the vast opportunities that await those of us in leadership as we navigate this world and offer vital, transformative, and vibrant ministry witness to a people who want to live authentically as they believe God is inviting them to do. For caregivers to the LGBTQIA community, this is essential reading."

—Neil G. Cazares-Thomas, Senior Pastor,
Cathedral of Hope United Church of Christ

"Whether it is developing a life-affirming ministry with LGBTQIA youth or attending to a 'what do I do right now?' pastoral need, Sanders's *A Brief Guide to Ministry with LGBTQIA Youth* provides a crash course full of timely and accessible resources for churches committed to loving and serving LGBTQIA youth."

—Kristen J. Leslie, Professor of Pastoral Theology and Care,
Eden Theological Seminary

A Brief Guide to Ministry with LGBTQIA Youth

Updated Edition

CODY J. SANDERS

© 2017, 2026 Cody J. Sanders

First edition
Published by Westminster John Knox Press
Louisville, Kentucky

26 27 28 29 30 31 32 33 34 35—10 9 8 7 6 5 4 3 2 1

All rights reserved. No part of this book may be reproduced or transmitted in any form or by any means, electronic or mechanical, including photocopying, recording, or by any information storage or retrieval system, without permission in writing from the publisher. For information, address Westminster John Knox Press, 100 Witherspoon Street, Louisville, Kentucky 40202-1396. Or contact us online at www.wjkbooks.com.

Book design by Drew Stevens
Cover design by Barbara LeVan Fisher, www.levanfisherdesign.com, and Erika Lundbom

Library of Congress Cataloging-in-Publication Data is on file
at the Library of Congress, Washington, DC.

ISBN: 978-0-664-26941-8 (paperback)
ISBN: 978-1-646-98450-3 (ebook)

Most Westminster John Knox Press books are available at special quantity discounts when purchased in bulk by corporations, organizations, and special-interest groups. For more information, please email SpecialSales@wjkbooks.com.

To my niece, Rylee—a living sign of hope

Contents

Preface to the Updated Edition ... ix

Acknowledgments ... xvii

Introduction and Terminology ... 1

1. A Brief Guide to Gender Identity and Expression ... 11

2. A Brief Guide to Sexual/Affectional Orientation ... 27

3. A Brief Guide to Ministry amid Questions and Crisis ... 45

4. A Brief Guide to Ministry with Parents and Families ... 63

5. A Brief Guide to Pastoral and Mentoring Relationships with LGBTQIA Youth ... 83

6. A Brief Guide to Queer Neurodiversity ... 93

Appendix: National and Local Resources for Supporting LGBTQIA Youth ... 101

Notes ... 109

Preface to the Updated Edition

The day after the 2024 presidential election, two friends of mine were getting their three children ready for school. They were watching news coverage of the election results when their seven-year-old child, Arthur, walked into the room on the verge of tears and asked his parents in a quavery voice, "Dad, Mom, will Donald Trump make bad rules?"

The question surprised them because they hadn't talked much about Trump with Arthur. They couldn't remember ever saying anything particularly negative about Trump or sharing their frustrations over the news in the preceding months.

Arthur's dad asked him, "What do you mean by bad rules, buddy?"

"Is he going to make a rule that boys can't wear dresses?" Arthur asked in a trembling voice.

This was even more surprising, as they had never talked with Arthur about Trump being unsupportive of gender-diverse people. Arthur is a boy who feels most comfortable wearing dresses. He doesn't identify as trans or genderqueer, and he is clear with anyone who asks that he is a boy who likes to wear dresses. He says plainly, "I'm a boy, and I like to wear dresses, so I want to wear a dress." Now he was concerned about the election's implications.

"No, he can't do that," Arthur's dad tried to assure him.

For Arthur's parents, this was a window into the stress that Arthur had been carrying during the election season. And it was an affirmation of how important it is to Arthur to be able to wear dresses. Arthur has a school where he feels warmly embraced and supported as a boy who likes to wear dresses and belongs to a church that also loves and affirms Arthur's gender expression.

This was the first concrete statement that Arthur had ever made of his awareness that wearing dresses may be perceived by others as different or problematic in any way. His parents never expressed to him any negativity or concern about Arthur wearing dresses. They told him that some people might think he is a girl so that he could be ready to explain. And they warned him that some kids at school may tease him, but that never happened. Arthur had not expressed any concern about what anyone thought of his wearing dresses prior to this day.

His parents assumed that kids at Arthur's school must regularly talk about the election. This is the only way they could imagine that Arthur developed a sense that anyone would have a problem with boys who wear dresses. They knew that Arthur's group of friends sometimes talks about trans issues, picking up on things from conversations overheard from parents. So, they tried to explain that adults whom he would see in the next few days and weeks are feeling sad and scared and unsure too.

Arthur's question that morning hit his dad hard. He teared up after Arthur left the room. His dad has a lot of queer and trans coworkers and processed the election with them over the course of many weeks. "This made the stakes of things more real for me," he said. "It made me feel worried."

Arthur's mom felt both protective of Arthur and a simultaneous lack of control. She said, "We can't really give him reassurance that everything will be fine, that he'll be safe." And she often wonders what the future will be like for Arthur.

The family lives in a great neighborhood, vocally and visibly supportive of LGBTQIA people. They walked to school the morning after the election feeling a sense of collective mourning, stunned and tired. And they know that the political climate is starting to become unsafe for their own kid, even while appreciating their strong and supportive neighborhood.

At the end of our conversation, Arthur's dad said, "It's really important for Arthur to be able to be accepted for who he is and to be able to express who he is at home." It is important for them as parents that their guidance and questions they ask of Arthur never be confused with judgments. Their aim as parents is "leading with love and acceptance of who Arthur is."

I asked Arthur's parents what they most wish people would take from their story. Most importantly, they affirmed "how valuable it is that your faith community is the place where you feel welcomed, and yourself, and safe, and loved." At their church, Arthur can wear dresses, and nobody thinks twice about it. People there notice and appreciate his personality. They are grateful that he's growing up in that affirming environment and that he will likely be surprised one day when he finds out that some faith communities are *not* supportive. Because a loving, supportive, affirming faith community is, happily, all that Arthur has ever known.

A NEW LANDSCAPE OF LGBTQIA YOUTH MINISTRY

Arthur wasn't yet born when the first edition of this text was written, and since then, the landscape has shifted precipitously. The political climate of today is vastly different from 2017's. And by "different," I mean much worse for LGBTQIA people in several discernable ways. It's evident that our idea of "progress" as an uninterrupted process of things always getting better is a comforting fiction. But it isn't descriptive of our political reality. Things do often get better—and they have for LGBTQIA people in many ways over the last few decades. And, at times, they get worse again.

The better: In 2011, President Barack Obama repealed the "Don't Ask, Don't Tell" policy, allowing gay, lesbian, and bisexual service members to serve openly in the U.S. military. Beginning in 2013, California and New Jersey became the first states to ban the practice of conversion therapy for minors, a psychologically harmful practice predicated on the assumption that gay and lesbian people can change their sexual orientation. They were followed by numerous other states. Then in 2015, the Supreme Court of the United States ruled that same-sex couples had a constitutional right to marriage in all fifty states.

Fast forward to 2025 as I'm revising this book for a new era of LGBTQIA youth ministry, we see things shifting for the worse and disproportionately affecting trans people:

—The new presidential administration quickly banned thousands of trans, nonbinary, and gender-nonconforming people currently serving in the U.S. military from service. All gender-affirming medical procedures for service members were paused, and currently serving trans military members were asked to resign from service in their respective branches.

—An executive order directed the State Department to no longer issue passports that accurately reflect a trans person's gender. Another order directed the Bureau of Prisons to deny incarcerated trans people gender-affirming health care or housing that appropriately reflects their gender identity. Another directed the Department of Housing and Urban Development to reverse its rules that gave trans people safe access to shelters. And a comprehensive scrubbing of all federal government websites deleted the mention of gender identity or trans people from websites and relevant forms.[1] Many of these orders were immediately challenged in court.

—Pertaining specifically to youth, President Trump issued an executive order to ban gender-affirming care for trans youth under age nineteen.[2] And another order attempts to instruct schools to deny the existence of trans people in schools, including banning trans students' use of the appropriate restroom, not allowing them to participate in athletics, and even forcing schools to inform students' parents if they request to be referred to by a different name or specific pronouns.[3]

—On a state level, at the time of this writing, the American Civil Liberties Union (ACLU) is tracking 604 anti-LGBTQ bills in legislatures across the U.S. that target a redefinition of sex, a ban on trans students using certain school facilities, curriculum censorship in public schools, healthcare funding restrictions for trans people, and a host of other proposed laws (70 of them have already been passed into law eight months into 2025).[4] In 2024, there were 533 bills introduced across the U.S., with 49 of them passing into law.[5] In 2023, some 510 bills were introduced in state legislatures, with 88 passing into law.[6]

You may be under the impression that young people don't pay attention to the news or aren't concerned about politics. But let the story of seven-year-old Arthur above correct your misperception. Even in a family that didn't talk openly about politics in front of the children, Arthur picked up on what was going on around him and in the larger political scene and was emotionally affected by the results of the presidential election.

The Trevor Project's 2024 study of LGBTQ+ youth mental health, which included eighteen thousand participants ages 13–24, found that 90 percent of LGBTQ+ young people reported that their well-being was negatively affected due to recent politics, and 53 percent reported that it was *significantly* negatively impacted. Nearly two out of every five respondents reported that their state's LGBTQ+ political climate had caused their family to consider moving to a different state, a statistic that increases to nearly half of trans and nonbinary youth.[7] And after the 2024 election, The Trevor Project's suicide phone and text lines received a 700 percent increase in contacts the day after the election.[8] Soon after, the U.S. Substance Abuse and Mental Health Services Administration cut its funding for specialized support for LGBTQ people in its suicide prevention hotline, which had been provided by The Trevor Project through the national 988 suicide hotline.[9]

While the political landscape for LGBTQIA people has grown more dire since the first edition of this book, we've seen discernable strides toward inclusion and justice on the ecclesial front. After five decades of policies that exclude non-heterosexual people, in 2024 the United Methodist Church removed all such restrictions and replaced them with affirmations of respect for the sexuality and gender identity of all persons.[10]

In 2022, the Reformed Church in America's (RCA) General Synod lamented the ways in which the denomination has failed to recognize the equal worth of LGBTQ+ people and the harm that this failure of love and compassion has caused. The RCA lamented the fear and frustration that has characterized their rhetoric on LGBTQ+ lives and affirmed the worth and human dignity of all persons, including LGBTQ+ people, as beloved image bearers of God.[11] And there's still room for the RCA to make strides toward inclusivity and belonging for LGBTQ+ people in order to move from expressions of lament to commitments of affirmation.

A denomination to which I have related, the Cooperative Baptist Fellowship (CBF), long refused to host a presence of the Association of Welcoming and Affirming Baptists (AWAB) at its annual general assembly. But in 2017, AWAB held its first ancillary event at a CBF general assembly, and in 2024 the CBF Affirming Network merged with AWAB, and CBF Executive Coordinator Paul Baxley celebrated the merger, noting, "Most conversations about matters of LGBTQ inclusion have been increasingly characterized by fear, demonization and dehumanization," while the merger resists this trend by "demonstrating a spirit of collaboration."[12] Now the Association of Welcoming and Affirming Baptists host a meal, reception, or concert annually at the CBF General Assembly in a packed venue. And, of course, there's still work for the CBF to do to end discriminatory hiring practices prohibiting LGBTQ+ people from certain positions within the organization.

The number of congregations publicly affirming the lives of LGBTQIA people increase every year. More queer and trans people are added to the rosters of ordained clergy in multiple denominations. More seminaries regularly teach courses in queer theology and LGBTQIA ministry practices. And while in 2017, this was the first and only affirming book on the market addressing LGBTQIA youth ministry (though there were a few non-affirming ones), now several other titles have been added to mine, aiming to equip ministers and laypeople to love and affirm the lives of LGBTQIA youth.[13]

WHY LGBTQIA-AFFIRMING YOUTH MINISTRY MATTERS MORE THAN EVER

LGBTQ youth who have at least one accepting adult in their lives are 40 percent less likely to report a suicide attempt.[14] I don't always find statistics inspirational, but this statistic, based on a survey of 25,896 youth ages 13–24, is almost *magical*. One affirming adult equates to a 40-percentage point reduction in suicide attempt! If you are trying to get beyond your hesitations about being an openly LGBTQIA-affirming presence in your community, please let that statistic push you over the edge.

If one affirming adult can have that significant an impact on the mental health and well-being of LGBTQ youth, then any time you spend sharpening your abilities to be a *visibly* and *skillfully* affirming presence to the youth in your life will be time well spent. Note: You must be *known* as an affirming adult for your affirmation to have an effect! And I know that seems risky to some in churches or denominations that do not yet affirm LGBTQIA lives, or that punish laity or clergy who hold affirming stances, or that believe that affirmation is a good thing as long as we don't make a big deal about it.

When I talk with churches about LGBTQIA affirming ministry, I used to ask audiences to consider how they would tangibly embody their love and affirmation for queer and trans people. In our current political landscape, I ask a different question: *What will you risk to stand in solidarity with queer and trans people?*

And I ask you this question, too. Right now, the demand is different than it was even a few years ago. LGBTQIA lives are being pushed to the brink by a politics of cruelty and violence. Trans people bear the heaviest weight of the current political ire. And LGBTQIA youth are by far the most vulnerable among us. We need straight and cisgender allies to come alongside us in the struggle for justice. We need denominations and congregations to *boldly* embody love and affirmation and belonging for LGBTQIA people and to actively protect queer and trans kids.

We need pastors and laypeople who will be open, *visible* representations of God's fierce and abiding love for queer and trans people made in the divine image.

We need you. Now.

What will you risk to stand in solidarity with us?

Acknowledgments

I am grateful to Robert Ratcliff and the editorial team at Westminster John Knox Press for seeing the value in a book like this and its potential to contribute to the health and well-being of LGBTQIA youth. I am also grateful to Jessica Miller Kelley and the WJK team for seeing the need for a revised edition of the book. I am especially indebted to Avery Belyeu, Sam Coates, Carra Hughes Greer, Keith Menhinick, and Davi Reese Weasley, who each read drafts of the text either in part or in whole and provided invaluable feedback that undoubtedly makes the book richer and more useful to readers. Finally, I am thankful to those who pick up the book and read it. There is really no other reason I can think of to read a book of this kind unless a reader is committed to learning how best to minister in an affirming way to LGBTQIA youth, contributing to their health, well-being, spiritual vitality, and livability of life. If no one else ever thanks for you for that commitment, which you embody in your ministerial practice, please accept my deepest gratitude.

Introduction and Terminology

Many lesbian, gay, bisexual, transgender, queer (or questioning), intersex, and asexual (LGBTQIA) youth now grow up in a very different religious context than did LGBTQIA people just a few years ago. Over the course of the past few decades, numerous congregations and some of the largest mainline denominations in the U.S. and Canada have progressively opened their doors to the full acceptance, inclusion, and affirmation of LGBTQIA people. How does an affirming stance toward LGBTQIA people affect the day-to-day experience of teenagers in the context of the local congregation? In what ways can a church's youth ministry have a life-giving impact on the lives of LGBTQIA youth who grow up seeking to live fully into the practice of their Christian faith *and* with a lesbian, gay, bisexual, or asexual sexual orientation or transgender, intersex, or genderqueer gender identity? How can a youth minister or youth ministry volunteer embrace, nurture, and provide skillful care for LGBTQIA youth in a congregation or community? These are the questions I address in this brief text, which is more of a "crash course" or "conversation starter" than it is a comprehensive education.

In this book, I assume a theologically and biblically *affirming* stance toward LGBTQIA people. That means that I assume from the first page that living out one's sexuality or gender identity as lesbian, gay, bisexual, transgender, queer, intersex, or asexual is fully congruent with living out one's identity as a Christian. While there is no shortage of printed resources to help readers develop LGBTQIA-affirming biblical and theological perspectives, there is a real gap in the available literature when it comes to practical texts helping ministers and ministry volunteers know how best to express these LGBTQIA-affirming biblical and theological perspectives within the bustling commotion of a lively, energetic, reflective ministry with youth.

For the purposes of this book, I aim to address concerns related to LGBTQIA "youth," which I am defining as youth between the preteen years and age twenty-one or so. Many of the examples and much of the discussion that follow will address youth who are middle-school and high-school aged, but the material contained in the book is also applicable for college-aged LGBTQIA people as well.

A GLOSSARY OF TERMS: SOME WORDS YOU *SHOULD* USE AND OTHERS YOU *SHOULDN'T*

The terminology surrounding sexuality and gender identity can be quite confusing. Even the acronyms commonly used for grouping sexual orientations and gender identities now seem like a bowl of alphabet soup spilling over the brim. Commonly, *LGBT* (or *GLBT*) has been used to denote "lesbian," "gay," "bisexual," and "transgender" persons. *Q* is often added to denote people who identify as either "queer" or "questioning" (of one's gender identity or sexual orientation). But the acronyms keep growing as we become more and more aware of those who aren't represented by our go-to letters.[1]

While the language is admittedly complicated and confusing at times, this complexity should be quite understandable. Culturally and religiously, we are emerging from a long era of LGBTQIA invisibility during which speaking of one's non-heterosexual sexuality and non-gender-conforming identity was, at the very least, taboo and could even make one the target of violence. As we become more comfortable talking in the open about experiences of difference and diversity in gender identity and sexuality, we start to notice our need for new language. Some experiences and identities are left out of our typical language, so we add new terms. Some words become confining and constricting, so we shift our ways of speaking about certain experiences. Words we once used with pride become adopted as words of abuse, and words once abusive are reappropriated as words of pride (e.g., the way the term *queer* has recently been adopted as a word of unity and pride rather than of shame and derision).

The following is a list of commonly used terms you might encounter in both popular and professional speech relating to concerns of sexual orientation and gender identity. The point of this list is not to provide you with an exhaustive glossary of sexual/gender language or to give the "right" definition of each term. New language is always being invented, and old terms go "out of style." Definitions shift and change from context to context and even from person to person. There were multiple changes to be made between the original 2017 and updated 2026 editions of this book, so know that this glossary will get you only so far in your language skills surrounding LGBTQIA experience.

General Sexuality and Gender Terminology

affectional orientation: A term often used alongside or in place of sexual orientation to indicate that "sexual" attraction is only one factor in a person's sense of attraction to another person. Affectional orientation highlights the emotional components and desires for connection that are an important part in a person's sense of romantic attraction to another person. Everyone has one of these!

ally: Typically, the designation given to people who identify as "straight" and/or cisgender but who support equality and justice for lesbian, gay, bisexual, transgender, and queer people. Being an ally is not an identity (like lesbian and gay); it is an *action*.

closeted: A term used to describe a person who is actively hiding one's own sexual/affectional orientation or gender identity from others (e.g., "She is 'in the closet' about her lesbian identity.").

coming out: A term used to describe a person's process of coming to self-acceptance regarding one's sexual orientation or gender identity and, often subsequently, making one's sexual orientation or gender identity known to others.

gender: This term encompasses factors beyond biology in relation to the presentation of a male or female identity; factors such as emotions, attitudes, and behaviors culturally associated with a sex of male or female. This term differs from the term *sex*, which usually refers to the biological components (e.g., hormones, genetics, anatomy) of a male or female or intersex identity. Everyone has one of these!

gender identity: A person's social, psychological, spiritual, and behavioral experience and expression of "gender" as male, female, both, or neither; or those for whom gender is experienced in a more fluid state not captured by the male/female binary. Everyone has one of these!

gender expression: The public cues and symbols that a person uses to communicate a gendered presentation, including such things as dress, mannerisms, behaviors, communication styles, and so on. A person's gender expression or gender presentation may not match the person's gender identity, as when a transgender person enacts a gender expression or presentation that is congruent with the gender assigned at birth, rather than the person's actual gender identity, which may be different from the gender assigned at birth. Everyone expresses their gender in some way, even if it is to defy male/female gender categories!

sex: This is a medically oriented term used to describe one's sex assigned at birth (see below) with categories of male, female, or intersex based most often on genitalia, though hormones, chromosomes, and other factors also come into play with sex. This is distinct from the term "gender," which encompasses factors beyond biology such as emotions, attitudes, presentations, and behaviors. Everyone has one of these!

sex assigned at birth: This is the sex—usually male, female, or intersex—that a doctor assigns to you at birth by looking at your genitalia. Everyone gets one of these. But one's sex assigned at birth isn't always descriptive of how one's gender identity will develop in life.

sexual identity: Sometimes used interchangeably with "sexual orientation," sexual identity describes one's self-identification in terms of sexual and affectional orientation and experience and attraction.

sexual orientation: This term describes a person's primary attractions and desires for physical, sexual, spiritual, or emotional intimacy. Sometimes, "sexual orientation," "affectional orientation," and "sexual identity" are used interchangeably. Everyone has one of these!

Gender Identity and Expression Terms

agender: Term typically used by people who do not identify with any gender or gender identity. In other words, *agender* describes those who are without gender or who are gender neutral.

bigender: Term typically used by people who identify with two different genders or gender identities (typically male and female, but not necessarily). These identities can be held simultaneously or they may shift at different times, as in the case of *genderfluid* people (see below).

cisgender, or "cis": This term describes the experience of people whose gender as assigned at birth matches their bodily presentation of gender and their own psychological and spiritual sense of gender identity. For example, if a person was assigned male at birth and the person's internal sense of gender as male aligns with this biological assignment, it would be appropriate to describe this person as a cisgender male. Prior to this term's creation in 1994, there was no term to use to describe the experience of people who were *not* transgender, transsexual, or intersex.

cross-dressing: A cisgender man wearing the clothing of and presenting as a woman or a cisgender woman wearing the clothing of and presenting as a man. It is *inappropriate* to use the term "cross dresser" or "cross-dressing" when referring to a transgender person who is presenting in attire consistent with their gender identity and expression. Cross-dressing is done more episodically and for a variety of purposes (e.g., for entertainment in "drag shows"), whereas transgender persons are not dressing across gender lines but are actually presenting as the gender they experience as congruent with their deepest psychological, physical, and spiritual sense of self.

drag: Used to describe a person of one gender (e.g., a cisgender man) who presents in the clothing of another gender (e.g., wearing women's clothing). It is important to recognize that "drag," "drag queen" (a cisgender man wearing women's clothing), or "drag king" (a cisgender woman wearing men's clothing) should be used only to describe this gender presentation as it appears in a performance, typically for entertainment purposes (e.g., a "drag show"). It is *inappropriate* to describe a transgender person who is presenting in the clothing of one's gender identification as being in "drag." Performing in drag has no necessary relation to one's sexual orientation or gender identity but is, instead, a gender performance.

gender normative: The behavior and presentation of a person that ascribes to culturally assigned norms for living out male or female gender.

genderfluid: This term describes people who do not identify with a static gender but whose gender identity and/or expression is ever-shifting. This shifting may occur in the ways they publicly present themselves in dress, appearance, or expression, or in the way they identify their gender to others and to themselves.

genderism: In contrast to the term *transphobia* (see below), genderism is less about "fear" of trans people and, instead, points toward prejudice—both individual and societal—against trans people, and to the social experience of injustice and oppression experienced in relation to this prejudice.

genderqueer: Often a self-descriptor for people whose internal sense and external expression of gender "transgresses," challenges, or moves beyond categorizations like male and female and who live against culturally assigned norms of the male/female gender binary. They may also describe themselves as "gender-expansive," embodying gender beyond the male/female binary.

intersex: People whose physical, hormonal, or chromosomal sex characteristics at birth do not fit neatly into the categories of either male or female but are ambiguous at birth.

nonbinary (gender): This term is descriptive of those who do not identify with the strict male/female gender binary. It may mean that they do not identify as gendered at all, as in the case of agender people (see above); that they identify with both genders, as in the case of bigender people (see above); or that they identify their gender identity as somewhere in between or beyond the male/female binary altogether.

transgender: People whose psychological and spiritual sense of gender differs from the social and cultural expectations attached to the biological/physical sex characteristics with which they were born (i.e., their "sex assigned at birth"; see above). Terms sometimes used to denote a transgender person's experience are "male-to-female" (MTF) and "female-to-male" (FTM). It is important to note that the general preference is for use of the adjective form of *transgender* or *trans* to describe a person's gender identity, rather than to use the term as a noun (e.g., one should say, "He is a transgender man," rather than, "He is a transgender" or "He is transgendered"). It is not preferable to use the term with an added "–ed" ("transgendered"). At the time of this writing, the general preference is shifting toward the simple term *trans* rather than *transgender*. When written with an asterisk, *trans**, it usually denotes a larger group more expansive than transgender people, e.g. nonbinary, genderqueer, etc.

transition: A term used to refer to the process that a transgender person undergoes to better align with one's gender identity. This may include any number of a variety of processes, including altering one's gender expression through choice of dress, mannerisms, behaviors, and so on (that is, "social transition"); changing one's name on legal documentation; undergoing hormone therapy; and, occasionally, having gender affirmation surgery to surgically alter one's anatomical sex characteristics (that is, "medical transition"). It is important to note that gender affirmation surgery is often not a part of a transition process for a trans person; it is only one possible step that a person may choose to take in living out one's trans identity. The term *transition* is preferable over other terms like "sex change."

transphobia: The irrational fear of or prejudice toward transgender persons.

transsexual: An outdated term applied to trans people who undergo gender affirmation processes, this term is no longer in regular use among trans people.

transvestite: An outdated term used to describe persons who engage in cross-dressing. This term should never be used to describe a transgender person.

Two-Spirit: This term is used by some Native Americans to describe intersex, transgender, or other gender-variant people for whom "male" and "female" gender identities are integrated into one person.

Sexual/Affectional Orientation Terms

aromantic: This is a term related to asexual describing people who have little or no romantic attraction or interest in romantic relationships. Some asexual people are also aromantic, but some asexual people do experience nonsexual romantic desire or attraction.

asexual: Used to describe a person who does not experience sexual attraction in any regard (straight, gay, or bisexual sexual attraction). This should not be used to designate someone who chooses celibacy (abstinence from sex) as a lifestyle but instead indicates people who simply do not experience sexual attraction as a part of their human experience.

bisexual: People who experience sexual and emotional attraction directed toward both men and women. This term speaks only to a person's sexual and affectional *attraction*, and not to how this attraction is expressed in relationships. For example, a bisexual man may be partnered to another man or partnered to a woman but still experience sexual and affectional attraction to both men and women.

demisexual: Sometimes used to describe people who do not typically experience strong sexual attractions, with the exception of the sexual attraction experienced on rare occasions to persons with whom a demisexual person feels a strong emotional bond. Emotional intimacy and bonding is the primary component of a demisexual person's sense of attraction to others, primary over other factors, like physical attraction.

down-low: Used especially in African American communities, this term is sometimes used to describe men who present publically as heterosexual (straight) but whose sexual attraction is for other men. This term is not typically used as a self-descriptor and is often used with a negative connotation.

gay: The most common term, at present, for same-sex attracted persons. This is typically used in reference to same-sex attracted men, with *lesbian* used for same-sex attracted women. However, in popular speech, *gay* is often used to mean same-sex attracted people in general.

heterosexual: People who experience their sexual and emotional attraction directed toward persons of the presumed "opposite" gender (i.e., men who are attracted to women and women who are attracted to men).

heterosexism: A term for prejudice—both individual and societal—against lesbian, gay, bisexual, and queer people, and to the social experience of injustice and oppression experienced in relation to this prejudice.

homophobia: The irrational fear of or prejudice toward lesbian, gay, and bisexual persons.

homosexual: Historically, this term was used in positive and negative ways to speak of those who experience sexual and emotional attraction to persons of the same sex (i.e., gay and lesbian people). Largely, *homosexual* is no longer used as a term of self-identification for lesbian and gay people. It has a cold, clinical ring and is now typically used only by those who hold non-LGBTQIA affirming theological positions (e.g., practitioners of "ex-gay" ministries).

lesbian: Women who experience their sexual and emotional attraction directed toward other women.

pansexual: Term descriptive of people who experience sexual or affectional attraction to persons of any gender identity or sex. Often, people who use this term as a self-descriptor reject the notion of a binary gender division between male and female and view gender as a more complex or fluid experience.

queer: The most common use of *queer* is as an all-encompassing term inclusive of anyone who lives outside of heterosexual and gender-conforming norms. So *queer* is often used to mean lesbian, gay, bisexual, transgender, and so on. But *queer* also has a more radical meaning, especially in academic literature, as a term that challenges the notion that sexual and gender experiences can be neatly categorized and understood in the fixed, static, and scientifically driven manner we have typically attempted to use in describing these aspects of human experience.

same gender loving: In many African American contexts especially, this term can be preferred in place of the terms *gay* or *lesbian* (see above).

straight: Another, more commonly used, term for *heterosexual* (see above).

Keeping Up Your Language Skills

Anyone who has learned a new language knows that you have to practice in order to keep up your skills. The same is true for keeping up your language on sexual orientation and gender identity. While the need for practice when learning a new language is to avoid *forgetting* the vocabulary and grammar skills you've learned, the need for keeping up your LGBTQIA language skills is due to the fact that the *language keeps changing*.

For example, some years ago, *homosexual* was the commonly used term for gay and lesbian people. Now, *homosexual* has a cold, clinical ring to it and is more frequently used by those who hold *negative* views about gay and lesbian people. It often carries a derogatory connotation in contemporary contexts. In the 1970s, *queer* would have been a term of derision, used abusively to harass gay people. Today, you may know teenagers who proudly identify as *queer*. Perhaps the most important lesson is this: language continues to shift and change.

So that your language does not become outdated without you knowing it, you might choose a few queer-oriented publications to read at least two or three times a year. For example, *The Advocate*, the oldest gay publication in the U.S., covers news, entertainment, and politics, and can be accessed in print or on the web. *The Huffington Post* is an online publication with a "Queer Voices" section offering news and commentary on LGBTQIA concerns. Websites for the Human Rights Campaign or the National LGBTQ Task Force or GLAAD are also helpful resources for keeping current in your language. These and many other publications can provide easy access to the most current language and vocabulary on matters of gender identity and sexuality. Accessing these publications at least a few times a year can help keep up your language skills, not to mention your knowledge of current events pertinent to LGBTQIA people. Even better, get to know LGBTQIA people with whom you can be in personal relationship. Nothing can replace the importance of personal conversation within trusting relationships.

Don't be nervous if this all seems overwhelming. You don't have to know all of the terminology in order to be an affirming presence in the lives of LGBTQIA youth. The best thing you can do if you are unsure about someone's preferred terminology for identifying their sexual or gender identity is just ask: "May I ask what words you use to describe yourself?" If the answer they provide is still confusing to you, a follow-up question may help: "Can you tell me about what that word means to you?"[2] This is much more respectful than assuming or guessing.

In order for your religious language to adequately match your developing theological understandings of sexual orientation and gender identity, it is helpful to keep reading books published by queer theologians and religion scholars. The citations found in the endnotes can help you to create your own reading list of books that seem most interesting and helpful to you in developing theological understandings of gender identity and sexuality and honing practices of ministry with LGBTQIA youth.

As you keep up your sexuality/gender language skills, remember that while "practice makes perfect" when learning a new language like Spanish or French, practice *won't make you "perfect"* in your ability to talk to youth about sexuality and gender identity. Ideas of "perfection"—not getting anything wrong, always using the "right" words, never having to search for the appropriate thing to say, never having to ask for clarity—will only make you so nervous that you avoid saying anything at all. Remember that this can be even more problematic than saying the "wrong" thing; your *silence* on matters of sexuality and gender identity may signal to youth that these are forbidden subjects to broach with you. You don't need to reach "perfection" in your LGBTQIA language skills. You just need to be intentional, attentive, and always willing to learn.

1
A Brief Guide to Gender Identity and Expression

Lydia has been an active part of the community at First Church since she was a toddler. She grew up in the church's Sunday school and when she hit the seventh grade, Lydia entered full force into the church's youth group, singing in the youth choir, serving on the leadership council, and never missing a youth retreat. Gregarious, smart, funny—Lydia is a youthful, energetic fixture at First Church, and her parents are a steady presence in the congregation's life as well.

At fourteen, Lydia is beginning to verbalize to herself some things that she has sensed in a more intuitive way since she was very little. Emerging into adolescence, Lydia knows that living life as a woman doesn't fit her experience. For as long as Lydia can remember, she hasn't felt at ease with the gender roles and expressions she was expected to live into.

Lydia has grown up in an era when transgender people on television and in the media are no longer a rarity, so she has identified with the experience of trans people she has seen on social media for a few years now. But Lydia also doesn't believe that transitioning to living life as a man quite fits her experience either. In Lydia's words, "It's not necessarily that I feel more like a 'boy'; it's just that I'm very sure I don't feel like a 'girl.'"

Since youth group at First Church is such an important part of her life, Lydia decides to speak about her experience to her youth minister, Jason. Lydia tells Jason all she has been thinking and feeling about her sense of gender, the ways that being identified as a "girl" don't work for her, and her uncertainty about how to live into her sense of self beyond this gender label. Jason is a bit taken aback, as he has never encountered any of these feelings and questions before in his five years as a youth minister. He has a ton of questions he wants to ask Lydia but realizes that this is her time to share what she wishes, so he just listens attentively, making sure Lydia knows he cares about her and wants to be helpful in any way he can.

A week later, Lydia stays after church on Sunday evening to talk with Jason again. Lydia tells Jason that she is sure about one thing at this point: living life as a woman just doesn't fit her experience. What she wants is to live in-between, not "buying in" to the gender binary. Lydia says, "I know that what eventually may feel like the best fit for me is making a more formal transition of some sort, but right now, I'm not sure that is what I want. I just don't want to present myself to the world as a woman anymore."

In the subsequent weeks, Lydia decides to be called Reed, a gender-neutral name that isn't confined to a female-identified gender identity in people's minds. Reed also asks her peers, teachers, family, and church community to use gender-neutral plural pronouns—they, them, their—used in the singular, to refer to Reed rather than female pronouns (she, her, hers). Reed's peers respond positively to this and, except for the occasional slipup, they honor Reed's pronouns. It is more difficult for the adult members of the church who have known Reed as "Lydia" for all of Reed's life and haven't benefited from the kind of intimate conversation with Reed about these decisions that Reed's youth peers have had.

Reed has questions for Jason about what it might mean for Reed's faith that their experience of gender doesn't fit what Reed has always been taught at church and at home. Is there really room for a non-binary Reed in this *faith tradition? Reed also has concerns about their parent's reactions to this news, which Reed is just beginning to share with them. Jason is concerned about ensuring that Reed's experience at First Church continues to be one that nurtures and supports Reed's spiritual life and faith development. He knows that he will need to seek conversation with others and read published resources to help him think through how to be the best possible youth minister to Reed.*

GENDER IDENTITY AND EXPRESSION: THE BASICS AND BEYOND

Gender identity and expression are aspects of *everyone's* human experience, though we speak very little about them—especially if we identify as cisgender. If *cisgender* is a brand new term to you, it's because we've talked so little about gender identity over the years that we needed to create a term to describe an experience for which we previously had no term. *Cisgender* is a word created to describe the experience of people whose sex assigned at birth matches their bodily presentation of gender and their own psychological and spiritual sense of gender identity.

The prefix *cis* is from the Latin word meaning "same"; the prefix *trans* comes from a Latin term meaning "across." Cisgender people identify with the *same* gender assigned to them at birth—with either the label "male" or "female."[1] Transgender people do not identify exclusively with this gender label given to them at birth. For example, if you were assigned the biological designation of "male" at birth and your internal sense of gender as male aligns with this biological assignment, it would be appropriate to describe yourself as a "cisgender man." This chapter aims to address the lived experience of youth who *do not* experience life as cisgender. In one way or another, these youth identify under the broad umbrella we typically call *transgender* or one of another cadre of terms to describe gender nonconforming experience. Reflected in this chapter, at the time of this writing, the language is shifting toward a preference for the simple term *trans* rather than *transgender*.

Gender identity refers to a person's social, psychological, spiritual, and behavioral experience and expression of gender as: male or female, both, neither, or those for whom gender is experienced in a more fluid state not captured by the male/female binary. *Gender expression*, on the other hand, refers to the public cues and symbols that a person uses to communicate a gendered presentation that includes such things as dress, mannerisms, behaviors, communication styles, and so on.

A person's gender expression, or gender *presentation*, may not match the person's gender identity, as when a trans person enacts a gender expression or presentation that is congruent with their gender assigned at birth rather than their deeply felt sense of gender identity, which is different from their gender assigned at birth. For example, a person assigned the gender of "female" at birth because of a doctor's interpretation of their genitalia, but whose *gender identity* is male, may live for a very long time *presenting* or *expressing* gender as female because there isn't sufficient safety or support or resources to live out a gender presentation as male. An example is the chapter vignette above, in which Lydia was presenting as a girl for many years, all the while not identifying in heart, mind, and soul with a female gender identity. Gender *identity* and gender *expression* can be at odds with each other.

It is important to understand at the outset of this discussion that gender identity and sexual orientation are two distinct aspects of our human experience. It may be helpful to go and do a little exploration of your own gender identity in relation to your sexual orientation using an online tool such as the Trevor Project's "Coming Out as You" guide.[2] This tool will help you to visualize how different identity categories are related but distinct aspects of who you are. Trans people, just like cisgender people, also have a sexual orientation: gay, straight, bisexual, asexual, and so on. Just as lesbian, gay, bisexual, and heterosexual people have a gender identity: transgender, cisgender, intersex, genderqueer, and so on. Likewise, we all have particular ways of expressing our gender that do not necessarily indicate anything about our sexual orientation. For example, a cisgender man whose gender expression includes dress, mannerisms, behaviors, and communication styles that society might typically categorize as "feminine" is not necessarily a transgender person, nor is he necessarily gay, as social stereotypes might suggest. Everyone has both a gender identity and a sexual identity, and these two aspects of our human experience intersect, but are not strictly tied to each other.

But are the designations "male" and "female" even sufficient to describe the experiences of our youth? In the chapter vignette, Reed experiences these terms as *stifling* rather than descriptive. Now I invite you to look beyond the male/female binary to understand more deeply the experiences represented among the youth with whom you minister.

Beyond "Male" and "Female"

For many of us, our cultural imagination for what *gender* means is transfixed by the designations of either "male" or "female." From the first chapter of Genesis, we've heard that God created the first people "male and female." Since this chapter intends to introduce you to the lived human experience of gender identity and expression for the youth in your church or community, we won't address all of the theological or biblical questions related to this concern, though there are helpful resources available on the subject.[3]

For a great many people, the very biological experience of life—even down to the chromosomal level—challenges the assumption that we can all fit our lives into this male/female binary. The identification as *intersex* (the "I" in "LGBTQIA") is descriptive of people whose physical, hormonal, or chromosomal sex characteristics at birth do not fit neatly into the categories of either male or female but are ambiguous at birth.

If you think this is too rare for anyone in *your* youth group to have an intersex identification, consider this statistic: Anne Fausto-Sterling's research suggests that around 80,000 births per year exhibit some anomaly in genitalia with approximately 2,600 of those babies born with genitals not immediately recognizable as either male or female.[4] Other intersex conditions are less visible and often go unobserved by medical practitioners until a person experiences a medical concern such as fertility issues.[5]

For many intersex people, doctors and parents will decide early on which gender (male or female) to assign to a child for whom these gender designations are not easily identifiable via physical characteristics. This medical practice has been challenged by intersex advocates. Often, it is only much later that the intersex person will come to an awareness that the "assignment" made on their behalf doesn't fit their lived experience of gender identity. Avoiding early medical intervention on intersex babies allows parents and doctors to follow the child's lead later on in life as a gender identity becomes more apparent to the child. The Intersex Society of North America is a helpful resource for understanding the complexity of these differences that exist from birth for so many people.[6]

When considering the lived experience of someone whose very chromosomes are neither XX (female) or XY (male) but, for example, XXY, XYY, or XXYY, we might wonder what it could mean for us *theologically* when Genesis 1:27 says God created humankind "male *and* female," which is how we typically translate that verse (emphasis mine). Perhaps the "and" in that verse takes on new theological meaning in light of the lived human experience of those whose very chromosomes betray the accuracy of the male/female binary we so often use to categorize people based on their sex or gender.

For others, the designation of "male" and "female" fits lived experience quite well, only the gender one was assigned at birth based on visible sex characteristics doesn't match one's psychological, emotional, and spiritual experience of gender identity. The umbrella term, *transgender* or *trans*, is typically used to describe people whose own psychological and spiritual sense of gender differs from the social and cultural expectations attached to the biological/physical sex characteristics with which they were born. All of the biological characteristics may communicate to doctors and parents upon birth the message, "this child is *male*," but this designation is made only based on what can be seen externally, not internally or chromosomally, and not accounting for how one's gender identity develops *psychologically* and *spiritually*.

When trans people come to the realization of their gender identity, *some* (but certainly not all) may choose to go through a process of *transition* at some point in life, a term used to refer to the process that a transgender person undergoes to alter one's physical characteristics to align with their gender identity. For some, this transition takes place at the level of gender expression—in other words, altering the public cues and symbols that a person uses to communicate a gendered presentation, which includes such things as altering dress, mannerisms, behaviors, and communication styles to match one's sense of gender identity as either male or female. This "social transition" may also include a name change and request for others to use different pronouns when referring to them. Others may choose to engage in a medical gender affirmation process involving hormone therapies or surgery when they are older, if such a transition is even financially possible. But no matter what type, *if any*, transition one undergoes, the experience of a person's gender assigned at birth not fitting their psychological, emotional, and spiritual sense of gender identity can be an important realization in the life of the youth with whom you work. As a minister or ministry volunteer, having some knowledge about how common this experience is can help you to become more receptive to youth who engage in conversation with you about their gender identities. No matter how small your congregation's youth group, you should never rule out the possibility that some transgender or intersex youth will at some point come through your church's doors.

Many trans bodies have been highly medicalized and put under the scrutiny of medical professionals—sometimes helpfully and sometimes harmfully. In the best cases, medical consultation leads to opening up possibilities for living life more fully according to one's gender identity. In the worst cases, medical scrutiny has resulted in stigmatization of transgender and intersex experience.[7] While a great deal of information exists in print and online to help you understand the physiological and medical information related to the experience of trans people, I will not address this research any further here.[8] Consider this a crash course in the medical aspects of this experience: what you need to know in order to begin to be helpful, *not* all you ever need to know about the subject.

Beyond the medical explorations, there are other ways of understanding trans experience, two of which are *experiential* and *theological*. These are the perspectives that I want to develop as we move forward, inviting you into more expansive and freeing ways of addressing gender identity in your work with youth.

Beyond "Transgender" to "Genderqueer"

It is typical for people to treat both transgender and intersex experiences through the lens of binary gender norms (i.e., male/female). But don't let what is *typical* limit your imagination for what is *possible* in the experiences of your youth. As Myra J. Hird notes, male/female norms suggest to intersex and trans people that "[b]ona fide members of society are essentially, originally, in the first place, always have been, and always will be, once and for all, in the final analysis, either 'male' or 'female.'"[9] Many individuals who are transgender or intersex do, indeed, identify as either women or men. Hird continues, "This identity need not, however, preclude the exploration of feelings of gender ambiguity."[10]

It is vital for those working with trans youth to recognize that the ultimate goal for every trans person is *not* necessarily transitioning through surgery or hormone therapy or any other medical intervention that aims toward helping a person "transition" from their sex assigned at birth to the presumed "opposite" sex (male-to-female or female-to-male). Many people experience themselves as either somewhere between male and female on the spectrum of gender or do not experience themselves as either male or female or anything in between. A term growing in use to describe this reality is the identification of *genderqueer*, which indicates an experience and expression of gender identity different from transgender identities.

For genderqueer people, the internal sense and external expression of gender "transgresses" or challenges or otherwise moves beyond categorizations like male and female, and thus, they live against culturally assigned norms of the male/female gender binary. Other terms youth might use to self-describe in similar ways are *nonbinary*, if the person does not fit into the male/female binary (similar to *genderqueer*); *bigender*, in the sense of having two distinct genders (i.e., being both male *and* female); or *agender*, in the sense of lacking any particular gender identity or expression. Still others may use the term *androgynous* to describe their gender identity and expression, indicating a sort of "sexless" experience and presentation of gender. Additionally, Nicholas Teich notes, "Children who are not labeled as trans but rather have gender expressions and identities that do not conform to the norms for their given sex may be called *gender variant* or *gender nonconforming*."[11] Many of these embodiments are often referred to collectively as *gender expansive*.

For example, in the chapter vignette, Reed was assigned the label of "female" at birth, as a child bearing the anatomical and, presumably, genetic markers of female sex. Reed was also raised as a girl, with all of the public cues and symbols that would tell others that the child is a girl (e.g., she was dressed in pink as a baby, socialized to use typically feminine mannerisms and patterns of communication). Reed, however, never experienced their own sense of self as female. But Reed doesn't consider transition to living life as a man particularly fitting to their experience either. Changing names, from Lydia to the more gender-neutral name Reed, changing pronouns from "he/him/his" to "they/their/theirs," and presenting a gender expression that is neither particularly feminine *nor* particularly masculine allows Reed to explore life between or beyond the gender binary.

Importantly, this living between or beyond the male/female gender binary doesn't imply any "confusion" on Reed's part. In fact, Reed came to this decision through lengthy, prayerful, deliberate exploration and discernment. While some within Reed's social sphere may be confused by *their* experience of Reed's gender expression, Reed is quite clear and may even come to use the term *genderqueer* to describe the de/gendered space that they now occupy.

Carra Hughes Greer, a veteran minister to youth and their families, helpfully adds to this discussion:

> Parents, and other adults in the church alike, often speak about youth as "experimenting" or "figuring things out" as if to say, they will test it and then presumably come back to what they consider

culturally normative. I think it is important for parents and others to understand that we are all always on a journey of self-discovery (e.g., figuring out career paths, sorting through marital relationships or divorce, our changing dynamic with our aging parents). We are living beings in constant change and growth—at no point in our lives are we static beings. Teenagers or young adults shouldn't be made to feel as if they are just "experimenting" and will one day not be a test subject. This quest for self-discovery should be thought of as normal and lifelong, ever changing, always fluid.[12]

Not only should genderqueer identifications not be an indicator of "confusion" on the part of a teenager identifying as genderqueer, we should also not view this gender identity as a "transitional" identity on the way to "fully" identifying as transgender—for Reed *or anyone else.*

Teich notes that a genderqueer person may feel genderqueer permanently; "in other words, it is not always a stepping stone to full transition. People can be perfectly clear that their gender is genderqueer, and that is how they live their lives."[13] At the same time, Teich notes, some people *do* adopt the label of genderqueer during a period of discernment as to whether or not they are going to make a gender transition from male to female or female to male. The important lesson for those working with genderqueer youth is never to assume this gender identity label is only a placeholder identity. For an increasing number of young people especially, genderqueer is an important and intentional way of living life between or beyond the gender binary in more gender expansive ways.

Theologically, we could wonder how trans and genderqueer youth help us to imagine the Divine in ways beyond the gender binary too. As Justin Tanis notes in relation to the Genesis text, "Genesis 1 clearly states that God encompasses both the male and the female since both women and men are made in the image of God."[14] The experiences and gender expressions of genderqueer youth help us to imagine and explore theologies expansive enough that God not only *encompasses* the male and the female, but theologies in which the Divine is also discovered in that which is *between* genders and *beyond* genders in our lived human experience. God, too, is gender expansive.

Beyond "Coming Out" to a "Call"

In their study of 3,474 trans people, Genny Beemyn and Susan Rankin found that a "sense of gender difference often occurred very early in childhood, when the respondents first realized that distinctions were made between girls and boys," and for 93 percent of all participants in their study, "they recognized themselves as being different from others of their assigned gender by the end of the teenage years."[15] For a majority of the trans people in their study, this emerging awareness of difference from their gender assigned at birth occurred before the age of thirteen. At the time that this awareness emerged, "most did not have a name for what they were feeling; they simply recognized that the gender that had been attributed to them was wrong or did not completely fit."[16]

Given these findings, if you are a minister or layperson who works with youth, you should be especially aware that this potentially important experience of gender difference is most likely to arise right in the midst of your teens' involvement in your youth ministry. While "giving" youth the language to use to describe their experience isn't necessarily helpful, *cultivating the space* for youth to enter into open dialogue with their ministry leaders, mentors, family, and peers about these emerging senses of gender difference is vitally important to the health, safety, happiness, and spiritual growth of your youth.

At the very same time, when youth—like Reed in the chapter vignette—enter into dialogue with family or ministerial leaders about their emerging sense of gender difference, it is important not to push youth toward a particular "outcome." That is to say, *never believe you know best what path your youth should take in their exploration of gender identity*. Like Jason in the chapter vignette, creating hospitable space, communicating love and support, and attentive listening are important ingredients in being pastorally sensitive and supportive to youth in the midst of gender identity exploration.

Another not-terribly helpful outcome of our strict ascription to the male/female binary in much of our religious traditions manifests when a youth begins exploring gender identity questions and well-meaning adults in that teen's life go immediately into action to "help" them come out and transition genders. As noted above, this isn't always the desired pathway for trans or genderqueer youth! Teich helpfully explains to parents (and to youth leaders):

> Tempting though it may be during a time of gender crisis in the household, it can be dangerous (not to mention extremely stressful on parent and child) to try to push a child into transitioning genders

simply because adults want to know which gender he or she is. . . . One important thing to keep in mind is that not all gender-variant children grow up to be transgender. In fact, most do not. This is another reason for parents to listen closely to their children and go with the flow, as difficult as that may be.[17]

It may be more helpful to think of "coming out" for a trans or genderqueer youth not as a one-time, definitive moment, and, instead, something more akin to the process of discerning a sense of "call." Transgender minister and theologian Justin Tanis explains, "Calling is about a way of being—a calling to awaken to, realize, and manifest who we are. For trans people, our calling is to a way of embodying the self that transcends the limitations placed upon us. We physically and literally materialize who we are on the inside and bring it to reflection on the outside."[18] Let's look at a few examples of such an experience.

When Izzy began to feel different from his peers, he was burdened with a sense of guilt and a feeling of being totally lost. When Joan felt that her life was not going to follow the pattern of her peers, she experienced such distress that it felt like she was constantly sinking—like a flood was rising around her at all times. It was almost as if Joan's life was slowing ebbing away. And when Zeek began dealing with his own sense of difference, he felt totally isolated, staying in his room most of the time. It was a long time before he was able to speak to anyone about his experience.

You may have caught on by now that these short vignettes describe not only the experience of trans people beginning to sense their own gender difference but also the call of the prophets Isaiah (Isa. 6:5–7), Jonah (Jonah 2:1–7), and Ezekiel (Ezek. 3:24–26) from the Hebrew Bible. As we consider how we speak about the emergence of trans or genderqueer identifications in the lives of youth—shifting from simplistic "coming out" discourses to "call" narratives—the similarities in these experiences are striking. The prophets, sensing a call from God, experienced fear and guilt; they hid themselves away and had the strong urge to run from their communities. Their distress was often so deep that they could barely get on with life, and they sank into states of depression and despair. Similarly, through their extensive research, Beemyn and Rankin found that the experiences for people of all ages encountering feelings of gender difference include confusion, shame, isolation, loneliness, and depression.[19] Note the similarity to the reaction of the prophets upon receiving a call from the Divine!

Casting such experiences of gender difference in the language of discerning a call, rather than a *supposedly* linear process of "coming out," may help youth and parents to see the journey nature of gender exploration and formation. It can be shocking to discover that one's experience of life is so different from that of one's peers. It may feel isolating to feel so profoundly different and, at times, not have language to describe the experience. It may even feel distressing and depressing to sense that bringing these realities into speech would put one on the margins of one's community. But cast in the language and narratives of a call, "rather than simply being a fluke, an oddity, or a source of shame," Tanis argues, "gender variance comes to be seen as part of our God-given identities."[20] Tanis continues,

> Even more than that, it becomes our spiritual responsibility to explore fully the nature that God has given to us. Like a calling, our sense of our own genders arises from within us and, at the same time, seems to come from a source that is beyond our control or volition. The sense of our own genders arises from within and without, from us and from beyond us. We know it in our innermost beings, and it comes from a source that is greater than we are alone.[21]

For faith leaders—whether youth ministry volunteers or ordained ministers—accompanying youth on this journey is a sacred task, full of potential for spiritual growth, developmental maturity, and clarity about the living out of one's gender identity and expression. The process doesn't always have the linear point-A-to-point-B progression that we imagine when we think of "coming out" stories. It is more often a process of discernment—like the discernment of a sense of call from a source that is beyond our control or volition. As Tanis says,

> If we are open to gender as a calling, then we will make prayerful and faithful choices about how we express our gender. We can select the expressions of gender that are right for us uniquely. We can combine these attributes in an infinite number of ways, and our medley of them is ours alone.[22]

Like Jason accompanying Reed in the chapter vignette, this process of discernment and exploration of gender identity begins with providing a safe presence with deep openness to listen to the experiences of youth on the journey, with no preconception of where a youth "should" arrive on that journey. Next, we'll explore a few ministerial practices that may aid you in the process of cultivating such space and accompanying youth in discerning their sense of "call" to live out of their gender identity and expression.

GENDER IDENTITY AND MINISTRY PRACTICES

How do we cultivate a youth ministry that feels safe enough for youth like Reed to live out their diversity of gender identities and expressions? How do we open space for youth to bring all of themselves into the youth group? How do adult leaders develop a nurturing posture toward youth exploring their sense of gender identity and expression?

One way of doing this is, of course, involving trans people in youth ministry leadership. If there are trans people in your church who have passion and gifts for service in youth ministry, inviting them into leadership is an important way of helping teens witness the gifts that trans and genderqueer people bring to ministry. Having trans or genderqueer adults in leadership also helps cultivate safer spaces for youth who reflect these identities in their own lives.[23] Imagine the possibilities for helping youth to see the beautiful complexity of what it means for humanity to be created in the image of God if we expand the images of humanity youth experience on a regular basis in our churches! For many churches, of course, this is challenging, either because of a lack of trans people in the congregation who can be recruited into leadership or because the church culture is still one in which LGBTQIA lives are not openly affirmed. In the following pages, I will explore two areas where youth ministry leaders in *any* church can begin cultivating the space necessary to invite youth to bring all of themselves into the room when they come to church.

Honoring Chosen Names and Pronouns

If you, like Jason in the chapter vignette, are privileged enough to have a youth come to you for conversation about their emerging sense of gender identity, you should feel privileged—*very* privileged. It probably means you've been doing a great deal already to become a trusted pastoral presence in the lives of your youth. If a teenager like Reed decides to trust a faith community enough that they can "try on" a new way of presenting gender expression in the sacred space of a youth group or congregation, that congregation is doing something to indicate to people that they will embrace gender diversity as part of the sacred tapestry of human experience.

As in the chapter vignette, the concern of chosen names and pronoun usage can be important in the life of a trans, intersex, or genderqueer youth. Once Lydia started going by the name Reed, they preferred to have peers use the pronoun *they*, rather than he or she. Some trans and genderqueer people prefer to use neopronouns ("new" pronouns) rather than he, she, or even they. Some of these you may encounter include ze/zir, xe/xyr, fae/faer, ey/em/eir, and ae/aer. Others prefer simply to be referred to by their names rather than with any pronouns whatsoever.

It is hard to imagine the profound meaning this may have for trans youth if you've lived your whole life as a cisgender man or woman, always feeling at home with the pronouns "he/him/his" and "she/her/hers," and never being called by a name you no longer identify with. But for a trans person, each time the wrong pronoun is used, it can feel completely invalidating to their physical, psychological, emotional, and spiritual sense of identity. Using a teenager's chosen name and pronouns—even when it's difficult to make a change after knowing them by a different name for many years—is an extremely important aspect of validating the sacred journey a teen is on in following their sense of call to live out their gender identity.

It is easy to imagine that some of Reed's peers will, at times, refer to Reed as Lydia and use the old she/her/hers pronouns because they've been referring to Reed that way for all of their lives as they've grown up with Reed at First Church. Importantly, youth ministry leaders can cultivate spaces in youth groups where microaggressions like this can be recognized openly, taken seriously, and corrected gently. Reed's peers may be so used to referring to Reed by the pronoun *she* that they continue to slip up and use *she* rather than *they*, as Reed prefers. They may even slip up and call Reed by the name Lydia from time to time, never intending to hurt Reed. Yet the experience can be deeply hurtful—a continual reminder that one's closest friends and family do not easily see what is becoming so clear to oneself about a deeply experienced sense of gender identity.

These mistakes are perfectly normal, and, while these inadvertent microaggressions may be hurtful to Reed at times, if Reed's peers and ministry leaders are intent on creating space for Reed to bring their full self into the church, they will strive to respect Reed's wishes as time goes on, practicing over and over Reed's chosen name and pronouns.

One practice to consider when attempting to cultivate space for trans and genderqueer teens is asking about the pronouns youth use, even when there are no trans or genderqueer students present that you know of. When you make name tags at retreats where new youth are present or you are combining groups with another church to hold a major youth event, encourage youth to write their names *and* the pronouns they use. When going around a circle for youth to introduce themselves by name, ask for their pronouns too. Not including this in introductory rituals can be a micro-invalidating experience, sending the unintentional message that gender-nonconforming or trans youth who may use pronouns other than he/him/his or she/her/hers—for example preferring the nongendered they/them—are invisible in the group. A person's psychological, emotional, and spiritual sense of gender identity is not always clearly evident based on one's visible gender presentation. So don't assume you know . . . *ask*! This simple act can go a long way in cultivating sacred space for youth to enter into processes of gender identity discernment and exploration in a youth ministry context.

Beyond the Binary in Youth Ministry Activities

"Okay, guys over here and girls over here!" Jason says as he leads his youth group in a game that he has grown up playing by pitting one gender against another. Then he remembers, not everyone in the room is going to be able to follow these instructions! He looks over at Reed, who gives Jason a snarky, exasperated look and then smiles as Jason blurts out, "Never mind! If your birthday is on an even date come over here, and if it's an odd date go over there!"

The ways we divide up our experiences and spaces based on the male/female gender binary are myriad. For cisgender people, it's hardly noticeable. But if you are in the process of transition, and don't yet feel that you've achieved your ideal gender presentation, these ways of categorizing experiences and spaces can become very uncomfortable. If you are living somewhere between or beyond the gender binary as a genderqueer, bigender, agender, or nonbinary person, having to continually categorize yourself as either male or female can be infuriating and invalidating. Even for cisgender youth, dividing classes and tasks and activities between male and female can limit what youth imagine possible for someone of their own gender—for example, the ways we've historically sent the message that math and science are "male" areas of inquiry or that certain artistic or caregiving tasks are "feminine" and not appropriate for boys.[24]

If you are a ministry leader in a local congregation, take a look at the ways you divide Sunday school classes of all ages. For young children, we may have one-room Sunday schools, but there may still be subtle expectations about which activities and toys are for boys and which are for girls. For youth, we may divide the boys' and the girls' classes, never considering where a youth like Reed will feel most comfortable. Even for elderly church members, strict gender divisions in our activities and classes leave little room for older trans adults whose visible gender presentation may prevent them from being able to comfortably select a class or activity when coming into your congregation. For example, consider the embarrassment caused to a trans woman who goes into the women's class and hears, "Excuse me, sir. I think you're in the wrong Sunday school class."

There are many other, far more *creative* ways of arranging our lives, experiences, and spaces than by strict adherence to a gender binary that does not fit the experience of so many of our siblings and sojourners in our congregations. Experiment with some of these in your own ministry and notice their potential for opening space beyond the gender binary in ministry. Here again, Carra Hughes Greer offers a helpful example from her own ministry, "The most rewarding way I split classes for Sunday school in our youth area is based on learning style and interests. For example, each week they can decide *how* they want to learn and discuss and experience the biblical text."[25]

Greer then splits classes into categories of "Create," in which students use art to experience the text; "Media," in which they use movies or other forms of media to view the text in relation to today's cultural context; "Discussion," in which a traditional lecture-based lesson is presented with time for extensive and honest conversation about the text; "Current Events," where students discuss the biblical text in light of current events in the news; and a "Prayer" room, where students use varied types of prayer methods and education techniques to understand the truths in the text and pray for the world around them, their peers, and the youth group. See how creative you can be in youth ministry when you move beyond, "Boys in this room and girls in this room!" Now go and do likewise!

2
A Brief Guide to Sexual/Affectional Orientation

Luke and Jasper have been friends for as long as anyone can remember. Both sixteen years old now, they've grown up together at Lake Church since they were toddlers. They are practically inseparable and are both leaders in the church's youth group—teenagers with spiritual depth and a commitment to follow the example of Jesus in their lives.

Since they were about thirteen, Luke has kept secret his developing romantic crush on Jasper. Not only that, Luke has also kept secret his attraction to other men in general. Since Luke is also attracted to women, he has only ever dated women and has kept his attraction to men to himself while trying to explore what this means for his faith and his future.

Luke is on the high-school baseball team—a group of teenage boys full of hyper-masculine zeal—and knows that revealing his same-sex attraction would result in being marginalized among his teammates. Though he's never had a conversation with them about it, Luke's parents are rather negative toward gay and lesbian people whenever the subject comes up on television or in conversations with their friends, which Luke has overheard. And at Lake Church, the conversation on sexuality and faith is altogether missing, creating a lot of uncertainty about how he would be viewed if he came out there.

Luke's questions about his sexuality, his ongoing crush on Jasper, and how all this will play out in his future as he begins to think about college now occupies his mind so much that he decides to approach his youth minister, Dianne, for a conversation. After he beats around the bush for a few minutes, Dianne can tell that Luke has something important on his mind. She asks him, "Luke, what's up? Seems like something is weighing on you."

Luke, not knowing how to bring up his questions, feels relieved to have an entrée into what he actually came to talk about. He begins to spill his guts to Dianne. He tells her about his struggles to understand what it means that he is attracted to both men and women. He asks her all of the questions he goes to bed thinking about almost nightly: "Does this mean I'm gay or bi or what? And what does it mean in relation to being a Christian? Is it possible to even explore dating men without sacrificing my friendships with the guys on the team or making my parents upset? And then there's Jasper . . . I know Jasper is straight—we've talked about sex and girls and relationships a lot before—but I have such a crush on him that I can't get to go away!"

Dianne has been a minister for about six years—much of that time working with youth—but this is the first time she has ever had a pastoral conversation with a youth right in the midst of questioning his own sexual experience. At least it's the first time one of her youth has had the courage to talk with her about these questions! She wonders, "Who knows how many other youth have had these same questions but have been too afraid to talk with me about them because I'm a minister or because I serve a church where these conversations just don't happen or in a denomination with a 'don't-ask-don't-tell' attitude?"

SEXUAL ORIENTATION: THE BASICS AND BEYOND

There are many models of sexuality identity development that attempt to describe the "coming out process" and other aspects of the experience of lesbian, gay, and bisexual people. These models often outline the steps and stages youth go through in developing an identity as gay, lesbian, or bisexual. These models can sometimes be helpful in understanding the experience of LGB people, *only* if they are understood as descriptive of the experience of *some* LGB people *some of the time* rather than universally descriptive of *all* LGB people, or, worse yet, *prescriptive* of a trajectory for developing one's sense of self through certain "necessary" steps of coming out.

The danger of thinking that there is a particular way an LGBTQIA person should come to a sense of self-understanding or "come out" to self or others is that the presumption of "a way"—with stages and steps that should be taken—forecloses on other possible ways that may be just as good, just as healthy, and perhaps more fitting to the individual's sense of self. So whether you are familiar with these sexual identity development models or not, I invite you to leave behind, for the time being, this linear, step-by-step thinking and explore the ways that sexual identity and experience are more complex than we're often invited to consider.

Beyond "Sexual" to "Affectional"

As theologian Kelly Brown Douglas says, "While sexuality is not the whole of who we are as human beings, it is basic to who we are. It compels our emotional, affective, sensual, and spiritual relationships. Sexuality does not determine all our feelings, thoughts, and interactions, but it certainly permeates and affects them."[1] As human beings, we are sexual beings, and that has implications for nearly every aspect of how we experience life in the world. Given that, many of the ways we typically talk about sexual orientation seem a bit limited.

Sexual attraction toward another person is only one of the many aspects of experience that draws us toward another in the lure of "attraction." Our attraction to other people transcends what we typically refer to as simply "sexual" orientation. Our attractions to others are, indeed, physical and sexual but are also emotional, cognitive, and spiritual. The term "affectional orientation" is now in use within the social sciences and points to the complexities of our attraction to other people, speaking to both the *sexual* and the *affectional* ways we are drawn toward another in the experience of attraction—with the fullness of our emotional and even spiritual experience. Sometimes the term "romantic orientation" is also used to describe the fullness of our sense of attraction.

Lisa Diamond, a psychologist who studied the sexuality of women over a long period of time, asked the eighty-nine women participants in her ten-year longitudinal study to describe their experiences of "attraction," which was met with such a wide range of descriptions that Diamond was unable to even compare them to one another:

> Genital sensations (*tightness in my groin; wetness*) to full-body physical sensations (*warm feeling all over; high energy, fluttery feeling in my belly; a sort of chemical connection*) to psychological states (*liking to look at the person's face or body; longing for nearness; not caring about the person's personality; wanting to have sex*).[2]

Diamond asks us to question whether all of these descriptions of "attraction" point to the same thing. Or is what we call *attraction* or even "sexual orientation" such a complex diversity of feelings and sensations and thoughts that to call it simply *sexual* is an oversimplification? At times, contrary to our usual way of speaking about romantic connection, a *sexual* component of attraction may be completely absent in the experience of attraction to another person (more on this below).

Think of your own experiences of attraction to other people—perhaps your spouse or partner or even an old crush from long ago. How did you experience your "attraction" to these persons? Describe the feelings you had when you first met them or when you were in their presence—physical sensations, emotions, thoughts about being with them, either sexually or otherwise. Perhaps you are beginning to see the complex nature of our sense of attraction to other people. When working with LGBTQIA youth, it is helpful to keep in mind the multiplicity of experiences that make up our sense of attraction to others and our desire to be with them in intimate or romantic relationships.

Sometimes churches have a difficult time talking about sexual attraction and sexual activity *of any kind*—gay, straight, or otherwise. As you begin making space in your ministry to address the complexities of human sexuality, you may also need to cultivate space in your church or youth ministry for the subject of sexuality to be broached at all without people feeling embarrassment or shame in talking about this important aspect of our human experience.

Beyond "Gay" and "Straight"

For decades now, we have, almost exclusively, identified our sexual orientations and those of others as either *gay* or *straight* (with *gay* including both gay men and lesbian women). But that simple binary of straight/

gay is quickly breaking down in its ability to describe the fullness of our sexual and affectional orientations and identities. The three major ways this binary fails to describe the fullness of sexual/affectional experience are seen in the cases of bisexual people, asexual people, and those who identify as queer.

Bisexuality

We often give voice to the fact that some people experience their sexuality as *bi*sexual—that is, attracted to both men and women—but too often bisexuality is put down by gays and lesbians or completely misunderstood by straight people. For example, for some time, gays and lesbians have wrongly labeled bisexual people as "fence sitters" who can't or don't want to "make up their minds" or "fully" come out as gay or lesbian, still hanging on to a bit of their heterosexual privilege. This is, unfortunately, a common example of horizontal oppression—that is, oppressive dynamics that play out *within* a marginalized group among its members. Many lesbian and gay people fail to recognize the legitimacy of the experience of bisexual people (who experience attraction to both women and men) and thus contribute to the stigmatization of bisexuality.

Straight people often simply misunderstand what *bisexuality* means and, thus, form perspectives based on false assumptions. Most common in my experience is heterosexual people who believe that bisexuality means that a person is sexually active or in intimate relationship with both men and women at the same time. Contrary to this mistaken view, the label of bisexual tells us something only about a person's experience of attraction toward others (both men and women) but doesn't say anything about how a person forms relationships. Many bisexual people are married or partnered to a person of the same sex, many to people of a different sex, and others are single.

In some ways, bisexual people hold up a mirror to anyone who identifies as straight or gay, calling into question whether that strict black and white binary really makes sense to *any of us* all of the time. Diamond asks this helpful series of questions concerning the nature of "attraction" in relation to our typical conceptions of bisexuality, asking us to consider what really "counts" as an attraction that is definitive of one's sense of sexuality:

> Do they have to be sexual attractions, or do romantic feelings count? How many different men and women do you need to find attractive

to qualify as bisexual? Is one single crush enough? Does it have to be current, or does a single attraction in high school (or elementary school, or college, or the military, or that yoga retreat you attended two years ago) count too? Do the feelings have to be long-lasting? What about a single erotic dream, a tipsy kiss, or several nights of deep conversation and intense fireside flirting during a camping trip? What is the role of sexual behavior? Is a person's bisexuality more authentic if she actually acts on her attractions? What about fantasies? Are they more or less defining than attractions? Does considering the prospect of same-sex relationships make a person bisexual or just open-minded?[3]

Consider your own experience of sexual attraction. Are there ways that these questions in relation to bisexual persons' experiences open avenues for you to think about your own history of attraction to other people, whether men or women or both? For many of your youth, these questions are far more commonly and easily asked today than they were some decades ago, and the identifier of "bisexual" is far more available and acceptable to many today as descriptive of one's affectional orientation. This is the case in the chapter vignette in which Luke questions his sexual and affectional attractions to both men and women. Hopefully, his youth minister, Dianne, will be able to help Luke explore these attractions and their relation to his emerging sense of identity in ways that will not stigmatize his attraction to both men and women and will not force Luke to speak of his sexuality in the stifling gay/straight binary.

Asexuality

While bisexuality is often still disparaged and misunderstood, the experience of asexuality is in need of even greater acceptance and understanding among those who work with youth. Asexuality is typically descriptive of people who *do not experience* sexual attraction. "The Ace Community" is a term sometimes used for those who identify as asexual. There are many myths and misconceptions about asexuality that continue to perpetuate its wide misunderstanding and that perpetuate harm toward those who struggle to communicate about their sexual/affectional orientation in an atmosphere of openness and embrace.

For example, many mistakenly equate asexuality with celibacy or a desire to be alone. But unlike celibacy, which is a chosen practice of abstaining from sex, asexuality is typically experienced as a deeply intrinsic part of a person's sense of self or identity.[4] Contrary to a life of solitude, asexuality doesn't mean that one wants to avoid intimate relationships. In fact, many asexual people do fall in love. Even those who don't enter into intimate romantic relationships still need their emotional and relational needs to be met. While some asexual people find it best to be unpartnered and have their emotional and relational needs met through friendships (sometimes identifying as aromantic as well as asexual), others find the prospect of being in an intimate partnership fulfilling of their emotional and relational needs.

Some mistakenly believe that asexual people are simply incapable of being *attracted* to other people at all. But many asexual people *do* experience attraction to others; however, this attraction doesn't have a sexual component to it, though it may still have a *physical* component of attraction to a person's *appearance.*

Others work under the false assumption that because an asexual person doesn't experience sexual attraction to others, physical intimacy is out of the question. But sensual, nonsexual contact, such as cuddling or even kissing, may be highly desirable to some asexual people. It is important to note that asexuality doesn't mean that one is *incapable* of having sex. Most asexual people are, indeed, physically capable of having sex, most just don't feel the need or desire to.[5]

For someone who identifies as a straight woman, for example, it may be easy to understand to some degree the experience of attraction of a lesbian. "Oh, it's like how I experience attraction to men, but she experiences those same feelings and thoughts and sensations about other women." For lesbian and gay people, it may also be easy to imagine what straight people feel for persons of a different sex. But for straight, gay, or bisexual people, it may be hard to imagine the experience of asexual people with empathic imagination—to really "get" what it feels like and to understand the experience of having no *sexual* attraction to other people.

That's why it is always important to hear the first-person narratives of those who sexually or affectionally identify in ways that may be unfamiliar to us, dispelling our inaccurate assumptions. An asexual man named Paul Cox recently described, in a first-person feature in *The Guardian*, his experience growing up. He relates his first experience of looking at pornography on the Internet, saying, "I wasn't disgusted or appalled—it was just boring, like looking at wallpaper."[6] When he describes masturbating as a youth, he says,

> It wasn't a sexual urge for me, I didn't fantasize, it was just something my body decided to do. . . . [I]f you're asexual you don't

necessarily feel an explicit connection between masturbation and sexual orientation. It's just part of having a human body—a physical, biological process.[7]

In the article, Paul also relates the story of meeting the woman who became his wife—she is also asexual—and candidly shares the details of their relationship when it comes to physical intimacy, interacting with family members and friends, entering into a committed relationship, and their decisions about the possible adoption of children.

One of the primary concerns with asexuality is that, for so long, we have not had the language and concept in our common, everyday speech for people to recognize their asexual experiences in relation to others with similar experiences. This sense of fundamental difference from others—knowing few, if any, who understand or know how to talk about this experience with you—can be isolating. Knowing something about asexuality may help you to better minister to those in your care for whom asexuality emerges as a fitting description of their sexual orientation. If you've never listened to or read the first-person narrative of asexual people, please access the article referenced above or the many resources available on http://asexuality.org.

Queer

For some, discovering a term to describe one's experience can feel completely liberating: "Finally, I have language to describe my experience, and there are other people with experiences similar to mine!" For others, however, all of the terms and categories we use to describe sexual and affectional orientation and experience can seem completely stifling: "Don't try to pin me down or box me in with these categories. None of them really fit for me anyway. Just let me be who I am, damn it!"

In some significant ways, this is where the emergence of "queer theory" has helped us expand our perspective on sexuality and gender identity over the past few decades. While *queer* is often used as an umbrella term for all LGBTQIA people, it is sometimes used more specifically as a term that defies easy categorization. In brief, Darren Langdridge explains, "Queer theory seeks to undermine this heterosexual-homosexual binary by actively refusing to engage with identity categories and actively affirming ambiguity."[8]

Perhaps you have a hard time understanding how affirming ambiguity can feel liberating, but for many youth in your ministry, the ability to identify (or perhaps *anti*-identify) in a way that affirms their experience of complexity and ambiguity in relation to their sexual and affectional orientation may be just what they're looking for. Identifying as queer should not be seen as a refusal to claim an identity because one is uncertain or unsure of how to label one's sexuality (people often use the term *questioning* to describe this). Rather, identifying as queer is an invitation to see beyond the restraints of our commonsense ways of categorizing our sexual and affectional experience with discrete little checkboxes and to embrace the mystery and complexity of our sexual and affectional selves. This constantly requires new language to be created, new concepts to be tried on for size, and new stories to be told from the depths of our human experience.

Beyond "Fixity" to "Fluidity"

Those who have long fought for gay and lesbian rights by arguing that our sexual orientation is an innate and fixed part of our biology have helped us to see the ways that more conservative religious and political calls to help lesbian and gay people "choose" to be straight run contrary to the experience of our sexuality. These messages of "changing" one's sexual orientation are, indeed, acts of violence against LGBTQIA people. Many who experience same-sex attraction have known something of our sexual identity for as long as we can recall experiencing attraction. Knowing this helps us to see our sexual and affectional identity as fundamental to our experience as human beings and has helped us to gain important rights that protect the dignity, health, and livability of life for LGBTQIA people. But seeing sexuality as part of our deeply embedded sense of being—our "nature"—yet leaving the discussion there, is far less helpful in really *understanding* the complexities of this distinctive sense of ourselves as human beings.

We are better served to think of our sexuality as an aspect of our identity, influenced by biology, for sure, but also influenced by complex factors of environment, psychological development, cultural backgrounds, interpersonal relationships, and, of course, spirituality and religious experience. Many of these varied influences have their impact on us far earlier than our first ability to name anything about our sexual/affectional orientation; so sexuality seems quite fundamental and even "innate" to who we are.

Langdridge helpfully encourages us that "instead of aiming for fixity, we should . . . aim for flexibility"[9] in coming to understand our own sexuality and the sexualities of the youth with whom we work. Instead of striving for the "right" *labels* to apply, we should be more interested in leaning into the *stories* that emerge. Instead of knowing whether or not the developmental model of sexual identity development is playing out as it "should," we can be more concerned that youth have the safety of environment and security of loving and affirming relationships necessary to ask good questions, tell important personal truths, and explore their experiences in relation to their spiritual and religious commitments. For many, these personal truths of sexual and affectional experience bespeak an identity that is more fluid than it is fixed.

It's important to note here that no matter the fixity or fluidity of a youth's sexual and affectional orientation, it is important to affirm that each person is God's good creation, just as he or she is or they are, even in the midst of great fluidity. We don't need a static, stable, or fixed sense of our own sexual orientation (as we've typically thought) in order to know that we are whole and holy and worthy of the love and embrace of the Divine.[10]

When we speak of sexual fluidity, we aren't just using a newer or snazzier term for bisexuality. Lisa Diamond, whose research on sexual fluidity in women is groundbreaking, says that bisexuality "can be conceived as a consistent pattern of erotic responses to both sexes, manifested in clear-cut sexual attractions to men and women (albeit not necessarily to the same degrees)."[11] Defined here by Diamond in relation to women's sexuality, sexual fluidity "means situation-dependent flexibility in women's sexual responsiveness. This flexibility makes it possible for some women to experience desires for either men or women under certain circumstances, regardless of their overall sexual orientation."[12] Simply put, no matter what sexual or affectional identity label one might adopt (gay, lesbian, bisexual, heterosexual, and so on), some variation in one's sense of attraction to others can be expected from time to time and from person to person and from situation to situation. In that way, sexual fluidity is distinct from bisexuality, which is an identification that a person uses to describe a typically *stable* and *persistent* attraction to both men and women; instead, it indicates that at one point in life, one may identify as lesbian but, perhaps years later, one may identify as straight or bi (or vice versa).

Diamond argues from her extensive research on women's sexuality that the sexual desires of women show more variability over time and across situations than do the sexual desires of men. Though she also points out that while some people—women disproportionately—are more variable in their sexuality than others, "*everyone* is capable of some sexual variability given the intrinsic flexibility of our sexual-response system."[13]

Another important factor to consider when thinking about our sexual and affectional orientations is how our attractions change and morph in relation to our romantic partners over time. This is especially important to consider in relation to trans people. For example, Tam Sanger helpfully notes,

> Within intimate partnerships involving transpeople, genitals are often decentered as the most important indicator of gender, and thereby sexuality. The sexualities of transpeople and their partners sometimes fluctuate throughout the trans-identified partner's transition (or both partners' transitions, if both are trans-identified) and sexuality may be based on genitals, gender, or something else entirely.[14]

This example from the lives and experiences of trans people is helpful in further illustrating the complexity of attraction that draws us toward others in ways that *trans*cend particularities of gender identity and expression and that may adapt and change even as our romantic partner's body changes through processes of transition.

From the chapter vignette, we might imagine a few years into the future when Luke returns home to Lake Church from a year away at college and has coffee with Dianne. Knowing that Luke already experiences sexual and affectional attraction toward both men and women, Dianne might not be surprised if Luke shares with her that he has mostly been dating women since being away at college and has sensed his attractions gravitating more and more toward women more exclusively. Or perhaps he shares with Dianne that the more he comes to understand his own experience, he realizes that while he is sexually attracted to both men and women, he is feeling his affectional and romantic attractions centering more on men and imagines that he most wants to be in a loving, long-term relationship with a man.

Rather than a once-and-for-all static fixity of sexual and affectional orientation, we should expect that some people may experience a fluidity of sexual and affectional desire that changes slightly over time or with variation in life situations. Knowing this can help ministerial leaders, like Dianne in the chapter vignette, respond with compassion, empathy, and understanding to the narratives of those who confide in us. Rather than treating such experiences as "confusion" that youth need help to sort out, understanding the potential for sexual fluidity can help youth leaders affirm the lives of youth whose experience transcends our limited preconceptions about sexual orientation.

While Diamond's concept of sexual fluidity can help us to better relate to the experiences of flexibility in sexual responsiveness that people share with us, we should not make the mistake of assuming that this means people can "change" their sexual orientation (more on this below). So, can one change one's sexuality through an act of will or prayer or pseudo-therapy? No. Does one's sexuality shift and change and morph over time through a confluence of biological, psychological, social, environmental, and spiritual factors? Yes, sometimes, for some people, and usually only slightly.

SEXUAL/AFFECTIONAL ORIENTATION AND MINISTRY PRACTICES

For at least a century or so, medical and psychological researchers have tried to categorize and define types of sexual orientation and attraction, using various measures and definitions for the subject of their study. As you minister with youth in your church or organization, I offer you this encouragement: don't try so hard to define and categorize your youth's sexual and affectional orientations and identities and experiences. Being able to pin down with scientific exactness just the right label for their sexuality won't help you be a better minister to youth in your church. What *will* help you be a better minister to youth is to develop your knowledge of the complexity and diversity of sexual and affectional experiences and to hone your skills at asking helpful questions to allow youth room enough to explore their experiences in a warm, affirming pastoral relationship (more on this in chap. 5). Before we come to these broader strokes of pastoral relationships with LGBTQIA youth, two concerns related to sexual and affectional orientation are especially pertinent to pastoral ministry with youth.

Attending to Multiplicity and the Intersection of Identities

Consider your own identity as an individual. How would you describe your identity to others? What "parts" make up the "whole" of your sense of self? Sometimes, instead of *identity*, people use the term "social location" to describe the varied positions we each occupy in society based on race, class, gender, sexual orientation, gender identity, age, ability, religion, and so on. Take a moment to describe to yourself your social location in all of these areas.

Most likely, you didn't describe yourself simply as a gay person or a straight person. If you really considered your sense of identity or your social location in the world, you produced *many* descriptors that are all equally true and valid descriptors of your sense of self and your location in the world (e.g., black, temporarily able-bodied, upper middle class, cisgender woman, bisexual). Pastoral theologian Joretta Marshall explains, "An individual's comprehensive identity is the integration of the various aspects that make that person who she is."[15] All of these ways of describing your identity or social location constitute the whole sense of who you are as a human being. So why is it that we so often speak of our lives and experiences and identities with one descriptor (e.g., gay) without considering how that descriptor relates to and interacts with all the others that we embody equally as much?

One reason it can feel so unpleasant to be defined by one characteristic of your being—whether it is your race, your sexuality, your gender, your age, or anything else—is that this one component of your embodied existence isn't *all* there is to you, no matter how important an aspect of your identity it is. We are all people with many intersecting identities comprising who we are as human beings. At the same time, when one important aspect of your identity is dismissed or left out of a description about you, it can feel like a major slight against the wholeness of your sense of self—as if that part had to be *overlooked* in order for someone to actually see you as a person. For example, "Oh, I don't see you as a black person, I just see you as a human." Or, "I never think about you as being gay, you're just so 'normal.'" Or, "Ugh, I'll never be able to refer to you with female pronouns. I just don't see you that way. I've known you as a man for too long."

Theologian Patrick Cheng uses the term "multiplicity" to refer to "a state of having multiple co-existing and overlapping identities, as opposed to a singular dominant identity."[16] This, he says, means that no single identity can become dominant over any other (e.g., black *and* gay, Chinese *and* genderqueer, working poor *and* trans). These identities are not mutually exclusive, and neither can our multiplicity of identities be separated from one another. "Rather, these identities are mutually co-constituted."[17]

In his book *Rainbow Theology*, Cheng gives specific attention to the intersection of race and sexuality. In it, he argues, "LGBTIQ people of color are not simply an amalgamation of race and sexuality. Rather, these categories are fluid and are inextricably intertwined with the other."[18] This is especially important for those who minister with youth to consider, as the youth in your church or organization are most likely racially and ethnically diverse or go to schools and participate in extracurricular organizations that are.

Let's say for a moment that Luke in the chapter vignette is a black student and Dianne, his youth minister, is white. Imagine that Dianne has done her homework and knows of a local LGBTQIA teen drop-in center that runs a peer support group. She encourages Luke to go and try it out as a possible affirming community. Dianne may not have even considered the racial composition of the support group and what it might mean for Luke, a young black man, to engage in vulnerable self-disclosure with others about his life and experience in a potentially all-white space.

Or let's imagine that Luke is Latino and is from a family with a father, uncles, and cousins who uphold a cultural ideal of *machismo*,[19] whereby Luke's self-disclosure of same-sex attraction may result in their loss of respect for him as a man. Rather than deeply listening to Luke's familial and cultural experience in relation to his emerging sense of sexual/affectional orientation, Dianne continues to encourage him with stories she has heard of other (white) youth coming out to their parents. Luke may go away feeling that Dianne just doesn't get it, because she hasn't taken care to see how Luke's gender, race, sexual orientation, and culture are deeply interwoven and not separate entities that can be discussed as distinct categories. Dianne may never have considered the ways that gender, race, and sexual orientation intersect one another and shape the experience of a young, gay Latino man differently from that of a young, gay white man.

We must become more aware of the ways that our identities are akin to intricately woven tapestries, where the threads of our race and gender and class and sexual/affectional orientation and gender identity and ability and religion and nationality and neurodiversity and a host of other identity markers overlap and inextricably weave together in multiple ways to produce a picture of who we are as human beings, a picture that is far more complex and beautiful than looking any one of these threads of identity in isolation could possibly portray.

Repairing Souls after "Reparative" Therapy

There is no more damaging practice wreaking havoc on the psyches and souls of LGBTQIA youth under the guise of "ministry" than the practice of "reparative therapy," sometimes known as "conversion therapy." These terms represent an attempt to blend therapeutic techniques and religious beliefs and practices in order to "change" a person's sexual orientation. Reparative therapy may or may not be performed by actual therapists, however; it may also be practiced by ministers and laypersons with no theological or psychotherapeutic training whatsoever. Many times, these general practices simply go by the term "ex-gay ministries."

As for the *legitimacy* of reparative therapy, the American Psychological Association, the American Psychiatric Association, the American Counseling Association, the American Psychoanalytic Association, the National Association of Social Workers, the National Association of School Psychologists, and many other organizations representing both medical and mental health professionals have all made explicit their position that "homosexuality" is not a mental disorder and is, therefore, in no need of a "cure."[20] Many of these organizations have issued statements about the damaging nature of reparative therapy and deem it an unethical practice for those holding clinical membership in these organizations.

Even beyond the mental health professions, many of those who have long believed in the practice of "ex-gay ministries" have changed their minds about its helpfulness. In 2013, the largest and most prominent "ex-gay" Christian group, Exodus International, shut its doors and issued an apology for the harm they perpetrated for thirty-seven years against the LGBTQIA people who looked to them for supposed "help."[21] Unfortunately, there are still many smaller groups—some that once operated under the Exodus umbrella—continuing to perpetrate this form of spiritual violence against LGBTQIA people under the guise of "ministry."

While it is important to know what mental health professions have to say about reparative therapy, I hope that this discussion will lead us to ask a new question: "What will churches, ministers, and lay ministry leaders say and do about practices like reparative therapy and ex-gay ministry?" Psychotherapeutic organizations have largely taken their stand on the matter. Now it is time for ministers and church leaders to see these heinous practices for what they are: a sinful form of spiritual violence against the vulnerable—namely, *youth*. When vast numbers of "ex-gay" programs operate as ministries and therefore work outside the oversight of professional bodies, licensing boards, and state agencies, churches *must* become more engaged in ending these practices in our communities and denominations.

Beyond your activism to speak out against reparative therapy and ex-gay ministries, many of your youth may very well be harmed by these practices and will need your caring support in the process of repairing their souls from the damage of "reparative" therapy. Theologian James Nickoloff helpfully points to a critical moment in the lives of many LGBTQIA people when he says,

> A crucial turning point in many gay people's personal journeys is easy to name: it's the moment when they recognized the fact that they had been lied to by all, or nearly all, of the people they trusted most—parents, other relatives, teachers, friends, newscasters, coaches, priests, political leaders. This shattering discovery can easily increase our sense of aloneness; at the same time it may propel us on the journey of self-actualization.[22]

At no point is this statement truer of LGBTQIA people's experience than when parents and religious leaders have encouraged—at times *forced*—an LGBTQIA youth to enter reparative therapy or ex-gay ministries to "change" or "repair" their sexual orientation or gender identity. Youth emerging from these programs soon discover—as the leaders of Exodus International finally did—that the ex-gay ministry is not effective at changing anyone's sexual orientation and, in fact, it inflicts a great deal of harm on the souls of queer folk.

As a youth ministry leader, it is important to become aware of the ex-gay ministry programs that operate within your geographic region so that you aren't naive to the harm being perpetrated on the souls of youth in the vicinity of your church or organization. Nickoloff continues, saying, "Although it is possible to recognize a lie and replace it with the truth, the untruth is never forgotten. Nor do we forget who lied to us. Whether the lie was spoken by one's family, one's church, or one's country (and then repeated by oneself), it always leaves a scar."[23] Some of the youth scarred by ex-gay programs in your region may—by Divine grace—show up at your door one day, in need of a supportive presence to accompany them in the healing of their souls from the harm of another ministry's sinful practices of spiritual violence.

The needs of these youth will not be uniform, but a general set of guidelines may help you think through what some of their needs may be so that you can prepare for this important ministry of soul repair:

—Be prepared to listen deeply and engage in conversation about a youth's image of God, which may be a source of deep pain if that image is one of a God who "hates" or "rejects" a part of their deepest felt sense of self as an LGBTQIA person.
—Be prepared to talk through passages of the Bible that may have been used by ex-gay ministries to convince LGBTQIA youth that their sexualities or gender identities are sinful and in need of repair. Have a few websites, books, and other resources ready at hand to provide to youth who are interested in their own exploration.[24]
—Be prepared to offer youth and their families referrals to local therapists who you *know* and *trust* to work in an affirming way with LGBTQIA youth. There may be particular traumas suffered at the hands of reparative therapists or ex-gay ministries that require the assistance of a therapist while you, as a ministry leader, accompany them as a pastoral presence (more on this in the next chapter).

The stakes are too high for LGBTQIA persons in our midst—whose *lives* are often, quite literally, at stake—for the most progressive of us to live in a comfortable, liberal bubble where we imagine such things aren't happening around us. Churches and communities of faith concerned about the effects of "reparative therapy" and other ministries intent on "healing" that which is not broken must develop the ability to think and speak and object *theologically* about the various forms of dehumanization that our theologies have often perpetuated. The lives of LGBTQIA youth depend on it.

3
A Brief Guide to Ministry amid Questions and Crisis

Heath has lived most of his life in a small, rural town in the southeastern United States. His mother and father divorced when Heath was very young, and his mother raised Heath and his two younger sisters with a strong adherence to a fairly conservative Christian tradition. For the past several years, the family has attended a small moderate-to-conservative church where Heath is heavily involved in the church's youth ministry.

Throughout his middle-school and early high-school years, Heath regularly attended youth ministry Bible studies and mission trips and exhibited a strong sense of identification with the Christian faith. This faith identity came through in his passion for dealing with the difficult questions of life and faith and in Heath's commitment to helping others through personal support and mission work.

Early in high school, Heath began to recognize that he was gay. As he entered his senior year of high school, Heath felt he needed to experience some congruence between what he knew about himself and what he was telling his family, so he decided to come out to his mother and sisters. Coming out as gay came as a shock to Heath's family and went against the grain of his mother's more conservative theology. Heath's mother vehemently challenged what she perceived as a "choice" on her son's part to lead a "gay lifestyle" and peppered her argument with religious language and Bible verses. Similarly, Heath's two younger sisters held to the guiding voice of their mother in shunning Heath's sexuality.

Not only did Heath's disclosure of his sexual orientation put him at odds with his mother and sisters, but also it soon resulted in his expulsion from his home. After being kicked out by his mother, solely on the basis of his coming out, Heath sought shelter in the home of a friend whose parents agreed to allow him to stay for a time. Unfortunately, his welcome at their residence ran short, as Heath's hosts had children of their own and could not support another teenager. Heath was able to continue high school for the month or so he stayed with his friend's family, but once he had to leave their home, he was forced to drop out of high school and move to another state to live with a family member who agreed to take him in for a while.

Throughout the multiple displacements forced upon him, Heath received little support from any adult in his church. Though he had been an active presence in the church's youth ministry and had developed a reputation as a young man willing to serve the church and others in the community, no one seemed to take notice when Heath became a homeless youth in a small town without a history of homeless youth.

QUESTIONS AND CRISES LGBTQIA YOUTH FACE

It is important to note that LGBTQIA youth experience all the same potential crises as their straight and cisgender peers, and not every question or crisis that arises in their lives will have its origin in their experience of sexual or gender identity. There are, however, a set of LGBTQIA-specific crisis experiences that point to the need for those in ministerial roles—whether lay or ordained—to develop competency in addressing with skill and compassion.

Coming Out or Inviting In?

How will the other youth in the group respond if a teenager in your church reveals his, her, or their LGBTQIA identity? How will the adults in your church respond to such a revelation? How will the larger circles in which that youth lives and moves react when that teenager comes out as lesbian, gay, bisexual, transgender, queer, intersex, or asexual? The wider community may include schools, sports teams, or part-time jobs, all of which may be places that will respond to a youth's self-disclosure of sexual orientation or gender identity differently. Youth considering these questions would be fortunate to have a trusted adult presence in their lives to talk through these decisions and disclosures.

One helpful starting place for those wishing to cultivate such relational space for LGBTQIA youth is to question the terms you've been given to understand such decisions. We've typically spoken about these decisions as being about the process of "coming out." The narrative we often have in our minds about "coming out" is something akin to Heath's disclosure to his mother and sisters—a moment of self-revelation about sexual orientation or gender identity followed by a reaction to the news by those who've been "come out" to. While "coming out" does often happen in this way, that linear narrative—along with the metaphor of "coming out of the closet" in general—is limited in its ability to open space for youth to live into their sense of self within community.

For others, like trans and intersex youth, the notion of "coming out" may not be a useful metaphor at all, as the goal for many trans people is eventually to live their gender identity without revealing that their gender identity may be different from the sex they were assigned at birth. Nicholas Teich says, "Some trans children are very open about their identities, but some want very much to blend in, understandably. So when they begin living as their 'correct' gender, they may stop coming out."[1] Thus, "coming out," while also a metaphor commonly applied to trans people, is limited in its ability to describe the importance of cultivating a community that appreciatively witnesses a trans person's emerging sense of gender identity as they begin to express it more openly in the world.

The typical "coming out" narrative presumes a linear process of development that begins with coming to some sense of sexual or gender self-awareness and progresses through stages to the point of revealing this self-knowledge to others. These "models" of development presume that a youth is moving in one particular, linear direction toward a certain identity that can then be expressed in a singular, clear self-disclosure to others. But this linear process does not always (perhaps, does not *often*) fit the experience of youth whose emerging sense of self is less *fixed* and *static* and is, instead, more *fluid* and *dynamic*. Therapist Julie Tilsen argues, "For queer youth who see identity as something they *do* rather than something they *are*, adherence to notions of development constitute a kind of spiritual violence, an experience of colonization into a way of being that does not fit with their own subjectivity or relational ethic."[2] Expecting LGBTQIA youth to simply "come out" in one singular, dramatic moment potentially forecloses on all of the ways that they might benefit from exploring their emerging sense of self within community, if such space is cultivated for doing this type of soulful exploration.

Challenging the ways that the metaphor of "coming out" places the burden of self-revelation entirely upon the LGBTQIA person, Darnell Moore introduces the concept of "inviting in" as an alternative.[3] Moore is attentive to the lived experience of "those LGBTQ persons whom for many reasons, such as socio-cultural, neighborhood, religious, or familial contexts, may find the process of 'coming out' to be more harmful than helpful."[4] Rather, Moore says that inviting others to "come in" to our lives "functions as a means of hospitable sharing, a choice to disclose to those with whom we may feel safe disclosing to, a choice to disclose when we feel ready to do so."[5] Rather than a movement outward (from the "closet," a presumed place of *secrecy*), inviting in offers others the opportunity to enter our "life-space" (a *sacred* place of honor for those we desire to be a part of that space).

A youth's process of "inviting in"—inviting you as ministry leader, peers with whom the youth forms community, teachers and coaches, or family members—is a practice of allowing certain, self-chosen others into one's process of identity exploration and discernment. "Inviting others in" is akin to issuing an invitation to those you wish to travel with you on the journey, not necessarily knowing the final destination at the outset. It may even be more akin to inviting others to *dance* with you; dances have no destination at all, only movement and music and beauty and flow. "Inviting others in" is an invitation to be *in community with*, rather than simply *coming out to*. Do you see the power in a simple shift in metaphor?

Julie Tilsen's counseling with queer youth is informed by the power of this metaphor, as she regularly asks the LGBTQIA youth with whom she works this question: "*Who would you like to invite in as guests to your world, where you can be a respected host, rather than having to come out into a potentially hostile world as an unwelcome stranger?*"[6] Youth may invite you in as a companion on the journey or a partner in the dance of discernment in order to help them figure out *who else* can be invited in as well. Youth may invite you in as a minister, before inviting peers or family, who they fear will not respect the sacredness of their life-space. Perhaps they've invited some in who have turned out to be harmful, and need help discerning how to renegotiate relationships with those who didn't respect them as hosts or who desecrated the sacredness of their soulful life-space with rejection or spiritual violence.

Whereas "coming out" presumes some form of finality, "inviting in" speaks to the ever-emerging nature of the process. It is a dynamic metaphor that reflects the more fluid and changing contexts in which youth will cultivate community throughout their lives. I offer this new metaphor of "inviting in" as a new lens through which you may see your own role in the lives of LGBTQIA youth and the sacred process of self-disclosure related to gender identity or sexual orientation. Know, however, that your youth may very well use the phrase "coming out" more regularly than "inviting in." There is no "wrong" language to use in relation to this process of self-disclosure. No matter the language used, if you've been "invited in" to the life journey of an LGBTQIA youth, you have the sacred privilege of companioning that individual in navigating this journey for many years to come.

Confronting Social Stigma and Bullying

No matter what kind of safe, hospitable, and loving space you create for the teenagers entering your church or youth group meetings, your teenagers spend only a fraction of their time in the context of your youth ministry. They spend a great deal of their time studying in schools, working part-time jobs, playing on sports teams, performing in extracurricular music and arts groups, accessing entertainment venues, and socializing in myriad public and online spaces every day of their lives. Sometimes the process of inviting others in fails to account for the ways some *force* their way into the sacred journey of LGBTQIA youth. Even if a youth hasn't made intentional self-disclosures about LGBTQIA identity, he or she or they may still become the targets of bullying and stigmatization based on a *presumed* LGBTQIA identity.

One helpful resource for understanding the current overall picture of school experience for LGBTQIA students is the GLSEN (Gay, Lesbian

& Straight Education Network) *National School Climate Survey*. The 2021 survey studied a sample of 22,298 students between the ages of 13 and 21 from all 50 states and the District of Columbia.[7] The survey found that 50.6 percent of LGBT students studied felt unsafe at school because of their sexual orientation and 43.2 percent felt unsafe because of their gender expression. Because they felt unsafe or uncomfortable in their school environments, 32.2 percent of LGBT students at the time of the survey missed at least one entire day of school in the past month. And 4 in 10 avoided gender-segregated areas, like bathrooms and locker rooms, because they feel unsafe or uncomfortable in these spaces.[8]

The GLSEN survey revealed that 76.1 percent of LGBT student were verbally harassed in the past year because of their sexual orientation; 31.2 percent were physically harassed by being pushed or shoved; and 12.5 percent were physically assaulted more violently by being punched, kicked, or injured with a weapon. Even when not at school, the Internet, social media apps, and texting opens the possibility for cyberbullying, a reality experienced by 36.6 percent based on sexual orientation and 31.8 percent based on gender expression. Many LGBT students, 61.5 percent, didn't report these activities to school staff because they believed that nothing would be done, or they thought that reporting the actions might make matters worse. Even more sadly, 60.3 percent of the students surveyed *did* report an incident, but reported that school staff did nothing in response to the report.[9]

In their large study of trans people, Genny Beemyn and Susan Rankin gave specific attention to the intersection of trans identities with racial identities and found that a "significantly higher incidence of physical assault was reported by transgender people of color than by transgender white respondents. . . . Thus, the combination of racism and genderism may account for the greater rate of physical assaults among transgender people of color."[10] They continue,

> Asked how they responded to the harassment, a majority of the participants indicated that they did nothing that would lead to the harasser being identified or prosecuted. The most common reaction to the harassment was feeling embarrassed . . ., followed by telling a friend . . ., avoiding the harasser . . ., leaving the situation immediately . . ., and ignoring the harassment. . . . Fewer than 10 percent of respondents confronted the harasser at the time (or sometime later), and only 6 percent lodged a complaint with the appropriate authority.[11]

If these numbers remain statistics on a page, they may not mean much to you. But these statistics paint a picture of school and community experience for LGBTQIA students in your church and in your community that summon your response of care and justice seeking. As the numbers indicate, many LGBTQIA students experience harassment and violence in their everyday school context, and too often they endure this violence in silence and isolation.

Consider the chapter vignette. While the story leaves out any indication of Heath's experience in school, imagine the painful and isolating predicament Heath will be in if he not only experiences rejection from his family but also rejection and even violence at school. In a situation like that, an understanding and supportive pastoral presence can be a life-preserving gift.

First, you should understand the experience of stigmatization and violence against LGBTQIA youth as a concern of care that goes beyond simply kids being kids. Stigmatization and bullying based on a teen's LGBTQIA identity has the potential to cut far deeper than kids picking on one another and can cause a range of potential harms. For example, Beemyn and Rankin note the many ways that individual perceptions of discrimination or a negative campus climate—namely in college, but certainly applicable for high-school campuses too—negatively affect student educational outcomes.[12] To understand how much psychological, emotional, and spiritual energy is required for students to deal with this type of stigmatization and bullying, it's helpful to see this as a form of violence that negatively affects LGBTQIA people, *even when it isn't happening in the moment.*

Iris Marion Young says, "Members of some groups live with the knowledge that they must fear random, unprovoked attacks on their persons or property, which have no motive but to damage, humiliate, or destroy the person."[13] Once LGBTQIA people experience this type of bullying or violence or even *witness* it, they may live with the constant knowledge that they are liable to experience this violence again at any time, completely unprovoked, and only because of their LGBTQIA identity. There's more on the effects of this type of violence in the section on LGBTQIA suicide below.

In addition to the careful listening and the comforting, supportive presence you provide for students facing this type of bullying and violence in their day-to-day lives, becoming an advocate and standing in solidarity with your LGBTQIA youth and their peers is a vital ministry of justice. One way to do this is to join with others in your community to become an advocate for safer, more LGBTQIA-hospitable schools in your community.

For example, do you know if your LGBTQIA youth have a safe and supportive space in their school? Only a third of the students in the GLSEN *National School Climate Survey* reported that their school had a Gay-Straight Alliance (GSA) or other similar club to support the well-being and inclusion of LGBTQIA students. When compared to those students who *did* have the presence of this type of club in their schools, they were significantly less likely to hear homophobic remarks, negative remarks about gender expression, or feel unsafe in their schools; and they were far *more* likely to report that school staff intervened in instances when these things did occur.[14]

Get to know your youth's day-to-day context the best you can, and, when necessary, bring together a coalition of others in your community to advocate for best practices in the contexts where youth spend a majority of their time. As you'll see below, these efforts will go a long way toward helping youth to experience their school and extracurricular environments as safer and more hospitable spaces. Unfortunately, schools are not the only places where LGBTQIA youth experience the precariousness of life caused by stigmatization, rejection, and violence. The home, too, can become the source of deep crisis.

Addressing LGBTQIA Youth Homelessness

LGBTQIA youth may become homeless for a number of reasons. Some LGBTQIA teens run away from their homes because their home life as an LGBTQIA person has become unbearable due to parental pressures to "change," or because of physical, emotional, or spiritual abuse in relation to their sexual or gender identity. Still other LGBTQIA youth, like Heath in the chapter vignette, are forcibly kicked out of their homes by parents who are unwilling to allow a child to live under their roof while identifying as lesbian, gay, bisexual, trans, queer, genderqueer, and so on.

The Trevor Project's 2021 report on LGBTQ Youth Mental Health found that 28 percent of LGBTQ youth reported experiencing homelessness or housing instability at some point in their lives, with the highest percentage among Native/Indigenous LGBTQ youth (44 percent).[15] The report also showed that 69 percent of youth reporting past housing instability and 68 percent current homelessness also reported engaging in self-harm in the last year, compared to a rate of

49 percent for youth whose housing was stable.[16] The disproportionate number of LGBTQIA youth who become homeless should cause shock, and should renew our vision of what it means to practice care for LGBTQIA youth in our communities.

As a youth ministry leader, ask yourself: If an LGBTQIA youth came to me to disclose that they've been kicked out of or have run away from home and are in need of help, would I know how to be helpful? Beyond a compassionate listening presence, would I know how to secure for this youth the shelter and services needed in the immediate short-term? Keep in mind that the average time away from home, parents, and guardians for LGB homeless youth is twenty-nine months, and for transgender youth it is fifty months![17] If you can't immediately answer these questions, it would be helpful to spend some time investigating resources in your area and developing a working plan of care in case this hypothetical scenario becomes a reality. The section in the appendix on "Homelessness Resources and LGBTQIA-friendly Shelters" will help you compile some of the necessary information and resources.

It is important to realize that you cannot assume, as so many do, that the LGBTQIA homeless youth in your area can safely go to the local homeless shelter and access the support services available to everyone else. If it is an adult shelter, it may be impossible for a youth to secure a bed. Even if it is a youth-specific shelter, only *some* shelters have developed competency to serve LGBTQIA youth, and—just as in their families, churches, and other social institutions—LGBTQIA youth often face discrimination and violence in the very places that purport to provide "shelter" for youth in need. If you want to be of support to the LGBTQIA youth who may, at any point, become homeless in your area, you must first get to know your region and what LGBTQIA youth-specific services exist near your congregation.

The Ali Forney Center in New York City, the largest organization serving the needs of LGBTQ+ homeless youth, provides an online listing of homeless LGBTQ+ youth resource centers organized by state and accessible via their website.[18] If you access this listing, you may note that several states have *no listings* available, indicating the extreme lack of services available for LGBTQ+ youth who are forced to leave their homes. Another national network of resources for ending LGBTQ+ youth homelessness is True Colors United's National Youth Forum on Homelessness. This project aims to identify and analyze policy that impacts youth at risk of or currently experiencing homelessness and advocates for policy based on their analysis and the experience of forum members, all of whom have experienced homelessness.[19]

If there are resource centers or shelters in your area, take the initiative to get to know these centers and those who run them. Ask how your church or faith community can support their work, through the donation of special offerings or of the supplies they like to keep on hand for youth (e.g., socks, underwear, hygiene items), or through volunteering. Programs to address LGBTQIA youth homelessness don't often have the funding and institutional support that other LGBTQIA rights initiatives receive, so there are always needs to help fill. Don't assume you know what they need from you! Take the time to listen and get to know the shelter or center, and be sure your offerings of support are understood as "no-strings-attached" gifts; some LGBTQIA organizations may be initially suspicious of what a church is doing at their doorstep.

If your community doesn't have a center or shelter serving the needs of LGBTQIA youth, then get to know the centers and shelters and services that exist for youth more generally (if there are any). Ask good questions so that you can discover whether or not staff is trained to address the specific needs of LGBTQIA homeless youth. Has the staff been trained in LGBTQIA cultural competency? Have past concerns of potential LGBTQIA bullying and violence within the shelter been addressed with a plan to reduce this type of violence? Is the shelter connected to a religious group whose teaching on sexuality and gender identity prevents the shelter from being an intentionally safe place for LGBTQIA youth?

Don't limit your investigation to LGBTQIA community centers and shelters. Figure out which social workers and therapists in your community have expertise in working with LGBTQIA youth in crisis. These professionals can be helpful allies to you and the youth you are companioning when times get tough. They are also potentially rich sources of knowledge about the community and social services for homeless LGBTQIA youth, which you may need to access.

Please don't wait until a homeless youth shows up in your youth group or until one of your own LGBTQIA youth gets kicked out of home to look for these resources! Know what resources exist before the need arises, so that, rather than scrambling to find resources to secure survival, you can be pastorally present and deeply attentive during the difficult leg of the journey on which this youth has invited you to journey with her or him or them.

If you find your local shelters lacking in competence to address the needs of LGBTQIA youth, begin building a coalition of community leaders—other ministers, therapists, city council members, doctors, teachers, parents—who will stand with you in urging the shelters in your city to develop the necessary competence, and to support them through the process of gaining this knowledge and skill.

If, after you've assessed your community and its resources, you find there are no appropriate shelters or services in your area for LGBTQIA homeless youth, find a few conversation partners and explore this question: What does your community most need in order to support the well-being and livability of life for LGBTQIA youth?

If your church is in a city hundreds of miles away from the closest place that an LGBTQIA youth can find shelter or assistance, perhaps you have the capacity for building community with partner churches and organizations, raising funds, and engaging in strategic planning for *founding* LGBTQIA youth services in your area. Start gathering folks together for conversation about the needs and possibilities: the other open and affirming congregations in your city, the local PFLAG chapter[20] facilitators, the counselors and social workers in your town with expertise in LGBTQIA issues, public school teachers you know who care about LGBTQIA kids, the parents of LGBTQIA youth in your congregation, and, importantly, the LGBTQIA youth in your congregation. It may not be an overnight shelter that you and your conversation partners determine your city or town most needs, but a daytime drop-in center where youth can come for resources and conversation. Or perhaps it is a publicly identifiable network of pastors, professionals, and public figures that youth can access when things get rough at home or they find themselves on the street.

Most important, don't limit your imagination by what you think is *possible*. When we are confronted with a problem as immense as the occurrence of LGBTQIA youth homelessness, our response must not stop with measured and reserved efforts but should extend toward full-bodied, soulful, and deliberately planned infrastructure to provide for the needs of youth in vulnerable and precarious positions. These efforts can be, quite literally, lifesaving.

Addressing Suicide among LGBTQIA Youth

At times, this precariousness results in not only lack of shelter but a type of "soul-precarity" that leads LGBTQIA youth to consider suicide as a thinkable option. The U.S. Surgeon General's 2024 National Strategy for Suicide Prevention, relying on CDC data, reports that 45 percent of LGBQ+ high school students report serious thoughts of suicide compared with 15 percent of heterosexual students, and 22 percent of LGBQ+ students report a suicide attempt compered with 6 percent of heterosexual students.[21] Of course, concerns about suicide are not just concerns for LGBTQIA youth. Suicide is the third leading cause of death among all youth ages fourteen to twenty-four.[22] Nevertheless, the prevalence of suicide among LGBTQIA youth is considerably higher than that of their straight and cisgender peers. And, at the same time, we must be quick to recognize that suicide is not a concern for *all* LGBTQIA people. Many LGBTQIA people live their entire lives never attempting or even contemplating suicide.

One analysis of twenty-five studies that included data on 214,344 heterosexual, and 11,971 non-heterosexual, persons revealed a twofold elevation in suicide attempts among lesbian, gay, and bisexual persons when compared to the suicide rates of their heterosexual peers.[23] In the Surgeon General's report, all studies considered showed 12–19 percent of lesbian, gay, and bisexual adults reported making a suicide attempt in comparison to less than 5 percent of all U.S. adults, while the numbers for adolescents is even more staggering: at least 30 percent of LGBT adolescents reported attempts compared with 8–10 percent of all adolescents.[24] While fewer studies have included transgender persons, the *National Transgender Discrimination Survey* reveals 41 percent of respondents (from a sample size of 6,450 people) reporting a suicide attempt.[25]

So while suicide is not a concern faced by *every* LGBTQIA teen, its prevalence among this population of young people is high enough to suggest that everyone working with LGBTQIA youth should have some familiarity with suicide assessment and prevention, as well as the dynamics underlying this experience for so many LGBTQIA people.

It is important to understand some of the dynamics at work leading to LGBTQIA people considering suicide as a thinkable option. In my own research with LGBTQIA people who made a suicide attempt, I identified several themes that are illustrative of the ways that religion comes into play in making suicide a thinkable option. Ministry leaders who regularly work with youth need to recognize that suicidal considerations do not arise in the same way for everyone. For some, there are mental health concerns. For others, extreme, distressing situations arise in life, making suicide a thinkable option. But for LGBTQIA people, there is often a religious or theological component to the consideration of suicide. For example, one of my research participants, a lesbian woman who attempted suicide in college, described the time leading up to her attempt in this way:

> I think when I'm talking about the core, that sort of inner sense—I think that's probably what I would call a soul. And that sense that, you know, as I was trying to own a lesbian identity, the sense that my soul was just sort of rotting was definitely leading up to [the suicide attempt] . . . like that sense that the thing that was my center, my heart, my, you know, connection to the divine was just rotting away.[26]

Her testimony illustrates the ways many of the religious messages LGBTQIA youth receive contribute to a type of precariousness of the soul that can grow to make life seem unlivable. The emotional and spiritual exhaustion alone, from having to constantly hide an important part of one's life, can contribute to this precariousness and to the feeling of being "hidden" and "trapped" with no way out. Another research participant described her experience of taking to heart the messages of her religious upbringing concerning her lesbian sexuality, saying,

> And these are things I thought because of my Southern Baptist upbringing and all those things I had heard preached from the pulpit and the scriptures that I had learned. So there was no way out for me if I wanted to be accepted by the church, accepted by my family, and accepted in the public. There was no way I could come out. Because I didn't want to be alone out there.[27]

The messages that swirl around us from a very early age—in church, on television, in the public sphere—affect us in ways that we don't always know consciously, but they become the building blocks out of which our sense of self is constructed. When these messages contain particularly condemnatory messages couched in language about "God's views" and "sin" and "divine punishment," they can be so debilitating to an LGBTQIA person's sense of self that they contribute to a precariousness of soul. Another research participant shared his struggle to contend with these messages that surrounded him growing up as a gay kid. He says,

> As a kid, if you're told you do something [and] it's an abomination, you can't tell the difference being told what you *do* is an abomination

and *who you are* is an abomination. I think it's impossible for kids. And the primary message about that was so concerned with whether or not you had sinned, that the fact that Jesus loved me no matter what, now and forever, was lost.[28]

So whether or not you are directly addressing a concern of suicidal thought, knowing how religious and theological messages can negatively contribute to the development of an LGBTQIA person's sense of self, or soul, can help you to cultivate ways of nurturing soul health for LGBTQIA students in your ministry. Nurturing the souls of LGBTQIA teens may include revising personal theologies in ways that are life-giving and that support the development of healthy and whole LGBTQIA identities, fashioning spiritual practices that sustain a teen's sense of connection to the Divine and to those with whom they share community, and even actively "transgressing" and challenging damaging theological perspectives that youth encounter in daily life in order to refashion theologies and practices that contribute toward the livability of life.

Beyond understanding the religious dynamics at play more broadly, it is important to develop a few simple tools that will enhance your ability to assess for suicidal intent when it presents in a caregiving situation with a youth. It is sometimes very difficult for caregivers to address others' suicidal thoughts and intentions, but being able to talk freely about these concerns has the potential to be lifesaving. So, if these conversations seem as if they would be difficult in the moment of crisis, then practice a few simple questions that you can keep in your repertoire when the time seems appropriate to use them. For example:

> "Are you thinking about suicide?"
>
> "Do you ever consider hurting yourself or taking your own life?"
>
> "Have you ever tried to kill yourself?"

Practice these questions regularly when you're by yourself. If you are uncomfortable saying them, practice more. Say them in the mirror, and watch your facial expression when you are saying the words. If you look uncomfortable saying them, practice some more until you appear less anxious and the words flow easier. Practice them with your significant other, a friend, and your colleagues in ministry—anyone who will play along with you so that you become more comfortable with the simple pastoral intervention of assessing a person's thoughts about suicide. Get really good at asking these questions and talking about suicide freely and with lowered anxiety. Becoming comfortable with dialogue about suicide could save someone's life someday.

Suicide researcher Shawn Christopher Shea describes what he calls the "triad of lethality": three indicators to be aware of that make death by suicide especially likely.[29] The first indicator of lethality is when the person presents with suicidal thoughts immediately after attempting a serious suicidal act that failed to result in death. Second, the likelihood of lethality is elevated when the person presents with a dangerous display of psychotic processes, noticeable when thought patterns are disorganized and behavior is extremely erratic. Third, the danger of death is elevated when the person shares suicidal planning or intent that suggests to you that they are seriously planning an imminent suicide attempt.

Confidentiality is always important in your work with LGBTQIA students who come to you to discuss parts of their lives they can't discuss with anyone else. When suicide seems imminent, however, *confidentiality must be broken* for the sake of saving a teen's life. Helping students to understand the need to involve family and other professionals in helping them to address their suicidal thoughts can be an important pastoral intervention. You can help a student navigate the process of disclosure; perhaps even help the student to express pain and turmoil in ways that will get the student needed help, without necessarily disclosing sexual or gender identity to family and social networks, especially if the potential of disclosing that particular aspect of the story seems to exacerbate the distress.

In situations when suicide is not an immediate threat but youth have had passing or occasional thoughts of suicide, contracting for safety with these youth can be a useful strategy. You and the youth create together a contract, listing detailed steps that a youth will follow if he or she or they ever feels at risk of hurting herself or himself or themself. For example, list a suicide prevention lifeline to call in order to talk with a trained professional 24/7, if suicidal thoughts arise. If this doesn't help, a second step on the contract could be calling you or another ministry leader listed on the contract. If this conversation leads you and the youth to believe further help is required, a third step may be contacting a medical or psychotherapeutic professional. Both you and the youth sign the contract, agreeing to the procedures you have outlined together. Youth minister Carra Hughes Greer, who has used contracts in her work with youth at risk of self-harm and suicide, says, "The act of writing the contract and going over it together always seems to give the teenagers I work with a sense of relief that someone is on their side supporting them and would have their back if they felt isolated and alone."[30]

In any instance in which you believe a student is at *immediate risk* of attempting suicide, you should know the resources available to locate help. In any situation in which you believe a student is at risk of ending life, *do not leave that student alone.* In extreme cases, when you cannot do anything to stop a suicide attempt, you may need to call emergency personnel (e.g., police and emergency medical services) to help. In other cases, you may need to accompany a student to a local hospital emergency room where psychiatric assessment can be made. At other times, when the threat isn't imminent, you may simply need to know the best psychotherapeutic resources in your community (e.g., psychiatrists, psychologists, counselors, social workers) to which to refer your student and the student's family.

Two national resources that you should know about dedicated to the prevention of suicide among LGBTQ+ and trans youth are the Trevor Project[31] and the Trans Lifeline.[32] Trevor operates a 24/7-telephone lifeline that youth can call for help, as well as a plethora of online resources for youth and those who work with youth. In the section of the appendix covering "Suicide Prevention Resources," you will find a partially completed worksheet of national and local resources. I invite you to consult the appendix and spend some time investigating other resources to support the well-being of LGBTQIA youth in your area, especially as federal funding cuts and restrictions impact care providers. Fill out this worksheet with the resources you find, make copies for other youth ministry leaders in your church, and keep a copy on hand for a time when it becomes useful to have these resources ready to share with your youth.[33]

If you work with a team of ministers and volunteers, holding training sessions on suicide assessment and prevention is vital. You may make up difficult scenarios—including youth struggling with suicidal thoughts—that your youth ministry leaders can work through together in role-play scenarios. Likewise, you may engage in similar training with your youth, who may be the first to notice that a friend who is having a difficult time is contemplating hurting or killing herself or himself or themself.[34] They should also know what questions to ask and who to go to for help if a friend is considering suicide. If you would like to have an outside trainer come in to work with your ministers, lay leaders, or youth, you can find a number of training resources available on the website of the Suicide Prevention Resource Center (SPRC).[35]

Making Referrals without Abandoning

Over the course of your ministry with youth, you have most likely encountered many pastoral concerns you are not equipped to address on your own. You need help either because the time necessary for walking with a particular teen through a crisis is beyond what you have to dedicate, or because the crisis or concern requires a certain skill set you don't possess. That's okay. That's normal. It is indicative of your ministerial maturity to realize when further support is called for that is beyond your capacity to provide.

When providing care in times of crisis—school violence or homelessness or suicidal thoughts—it can be very important to connect youth with professionals who can help address the critical needs of the situation. Carra Hughes Greer explains the importance of choosing words wisely when helping youth engage resources beyond the minister or youth ministry volunteer. She says, "It is important to convey to the youth you are not 'getting rid' of them. You still want to be a part of their journey and experience as much as they allow, but you, as the minister, have a network you want to share with this teen, too."[36]

Rather than the clinical-sounding *referral*, pastoral theologian Wayne Oates thinks of this as the "ministry of introduction."[37] When engaging in the ministry of introduction, you aren't passing an LGBTQIA youth off to another professional when your abilities to help run out—because the problem is "too big" or because you don't have the time to deal with it. You are prayerfully and intentionally introducing this youth to another caring professional or community that can help to provide for the teen's needs in specialized ways *alongside* the caring, pastoral presence you continue to provide for that youth.

4
A Brief Guide to Ministry with Parents and Families

Brian and Allison arrive unannounced at the office of their pastor, Rev. Emilie. She invites the couple in to talk, noticing they seem a bit distressed. Not knowing exactly what they are here to discuss, but having some inkling, Rev. Emilie is more than a little nervous. Just a few weeks ago, Brian and Allison's son and only child, Patrick, came to Rev. Emilie for advice.

Patrick, seventeen years old and nearing graduation from high school, explained that he has known for some time that he is attracted to other men. Patrick has never dated other men or dated much at all, really. He's taken a couple of his female peers to school dances, but never been interested in them romantically. Patrick sees college as an opportunity to possibly explore dating men for the first time. He graduates high school in fewer than two months, and at the end of the summer will be moving a couple of hours' drive from home to attend school. Patrick has resolved many of the questions he's had about his sexuality over the years, mostly through reading and exploration in conversation with a couple of close friends he has invited into this part of his journey. But he hasn't yet decided whether telling his parents about his sexual orientation is a good idea or not. As an only child, he's always been close to them and doesn't want to keep this important part of his life from them any longer; but he's nervous about it.

Throughout the conversation, Rev. Emilie asked Patrick questions like, "How do you imagine that conversation going with your parents? What are your best hopes for how your parents will respond? What are the fears that speak to you words of caution about inviting them in? What will change about your day-to-day life if your best hopes come true? What might change if your fearful words of caution are correct?"

Patrick replied, "I really hope they'll say they already know and that everything will be fine. I know they love me, I'm just nervous about disappointing them in some way."

Rev. Emilie helped Patrick to think through the ways a negative reaction could impact their relationship and to imagine how a conversation about his affectional orientation might get started. "Should I just sit down with my parents and have a conversation?" Patrick asked. "I don't know if I want to see their reaction! Maybe I should just write them a letter and get it all out first and then follow up with them later?" Rev. Emilie helped him think about what both of those options would feel like to him.

When they left the conversation, Patrick expressed a deep sense of relief to be able to talk about this decision with someone who knows both Patrick and his parents so well—few other adults would. But upon leaving, he was still uncertain about what he would do. When Brian and Allison show up at the door, however, Rev. Emilie is pretty sure what he had decided.

Brian and Allison tell Rev. Emilie they know Patrick spoke with her, and they thank her for being supportive to him. But they also express their deep disappointment in finding out that their son is attracted to other men. They're questioning whether it's even a good idea for Patrick to go off to college so far away. "We know it's his dream school, but I'm afraid of the trouble he could get into with all of this," Brian says. "And what if he gets attacked or something and we weren't there to help him? This is still a pretty conservative part of the country, you know." Rev. Emilie notes aloud that Brian seems both concerned about what his son's sexuality will mean for his future but also concerned for his safety and well-being, as any caring parent would be.

In the course of the conversation, Allison reveals she really isn't as upset by Patrick's disclosure as Brian is. "In some sense, I don't know—intuitively, I guess—I think I've always known," she says. "I mean, I'm his mother!"

Brian says that he not only didn't know but also doesn't quite believe how it can be true. "It's almost all I can think about since he told us a few days ago. I just want to talk it out with him and make sure he sees why this is not such a good idea for his future," Brian says.

Allison says it's been the topic of conversation at every meal since Patrick told them. Patrick has become less talkative and more withdrawn, spending more time away from the house. "I think it's because we're bombarding him with our questions and concerns," she says. But Brian is insistent that they "shouldn't just let this go on" until he ships off to college in a couple of months.

Rev. Emilie can imagine what this constant conversation must feel like to Patrick, and she offers this invitation to Brian and Allison: "Brian and Allison, from what you've told me, I imagine that Patrick has come to understand your hesitations and concerns about his sexual identity. But it also seems that those perspectives have taken over your family time as the primary topic of discussion at every family meal or outing. Brian, I wonder if you could be satisfied, for the time being, knowing that Patrick probably understands where you are coming from on the matter and allow some space for other conversational pathways to emerge."

Brian agrees he needs to stop making Patrick's sexuality the only topic they discuss when they're together. "I'm just having a hard time with this idea that he's not going to go get an education and meet a beautiful woman whom he'll marry and start a good career and have a lot of grandkids for us. It's just how I've always pictured things going in my mind."

Rev. Emilie poses a simple question: "I wonder if you can imagine what life might be like for Patrick if he meets a man with whom he falls in love."

"I really haven't thought about it," Brian says.

> "I have," Allison replies. "I think it could be beautiful. And we may still have grandkids!"
>
> Rev. Emilie encourages Allison and Brian to let go of some of their previous patterns of critical questioning for a while and become a little more compassionately curious about how Patrick imagines his life over the next few years in college and even beyond. They agree that might be nice to hear, as they've been so focused on getting their perspectives across to Patrick that they haven't really heard his hopes and dreams.
>
> As Brian and Allison leave the office, Rev. Emilie makes a note to check in with Patrick in a day or so to see how this experience has been for him.

My primary goal in this chapter is to help you think through some important areas of ministry in order to support parents and families in supporting their LGBTQIA youth. I will state up front, however, that while the well-being of the family as a whole is vital, *the LGBTQIA youth's well-being is your primary pastoral and ethical concern.* I take seriously the biblical mandate throughout Scripture to ascribe primary importance to the well-being of the most vulnerable. In a family, the LGBTQIA youth occupies that position of *most* vulnerability. These youth are vulnerable in at least two ways: their minority sexual or gender identity often means they are targets of rejection and violence; and they are vulnerable due to their status as a minor, which indicates a heavy reliance on the resources of family for their very survival and well-being.

The Family Acceptance Project's[1] research found that adolescents self-identify as lesbian, gay, or bisexual, on average, at age 13.4; while parents and families report their children identifying as gay even earlier than this—anywhere between 7 and 12 years of age.[2] For trans kids, the age of their gender-identity presentation is often even earlier. As a recent Substance Abuse and Mental Health Services Administration (SAMHSA) report notes, "Because children can express a clear sense of gender identity at very early ages, many are able to communicate their experiences to parents and caregivers, so there is greater awareness among some families that a child or adolescent might be transgender."[3] These numbers paint a pretty clear picture of the importance of your work with parents and families of LGBTQIA youth. What follows are several elements of ministry with these parents and families that I hope will help you develop your pastoral skills in this area.

HELPING YOUTH INVITE PARENTS AND FAMILY IN

Given the earlier ages at which youth are disclosing LGBTQIA identities to their parents and families, and the implications for family acceptance/rejection on the health and well-being of youth, it is imperative for those who work with youth to become prepared to help LGBTQIA youth navigate this process of what some call "coming out" and what we've been thinking about in this book as "inviting in." Many families who simply will not turn to a therapist or support group to explore their questions related to their LGBTQIA child or youth *will* turn to their minister, whom they trust and see on a regular basis.

As you embark on these important conversations with LGBTQIA youth, remember Tilsen's key question from chapter 4 about the process of inviting in: "*Who would you like to invite in as guests to your world, where you can be a respected host, rather than having to come out into a potentially hostile world as an unwelcome stranger?*"[4] This shifts the power of the traditional "coming out" narrative, in which an LGBTQIA person enters a position of vulnerability by revealing something deeply personal to people who may respond negatively. Instead, you may think of yourself as helping LGBTQIA youth consider how to invite family members *into* an important area of the youths' lives, *sacred* places of honor for those they desire to be a part of those spaces.

The most vital thing to remember in the process of working with the families of LGBTQIA youth is this: in the process of "inviting family in," the LGBTQIA youth are always the hosts—deciding *who* to invite in, and *when, how quickly*, and with what *level of access* to the sacred spaces of their hearts and souls. But even as the LGBTQIA youth are hosts in this process, they may appreciate someone like you—youth ministry leader, mentor, pastor, friend—helping them through the decision-making process as a supportive, affirming, and stable presence.

As you work with LGBTQIA youth to discern who to invite in to their sacred journeys, refrain from trying to step into the host role, making too many strong suggestions about who should be invited in and when. Asking helpful questions is preferable to giving strong advice. Given the economic dependence youth have on their families, it should come as no surprise that many LGBTQIA youth may choose not to invite parents and family into their unfolding journeys of sexual and gender identity, if they fear it could mean being kicked out of the home, cut off financially (e.g., if the family is currently paying for college tuition), or cut off emotionally. Helping youth think through these questions may look something like what Rev. Emilie did with Patrick in the chapter vignette, asking: "What are your best hopes for how your parents will respond? What are the fears that speak to you words of caution about inviting them in? What will change about your day-to-day life if your best hopes are true? What might change if your fearful words of caution are correct?" These questions help to carefully discern and assess both the emotional and the material implications of the decision Patrick is making. Some may choose to proceed with the invitation and others may rightfully see delaying the invitation as the best option for their overall well-being.

Considering the fluidity of identity addressed in previous chapters and "queer" refusals to align with strict binary (male/female, gay/straight) identity categories, Tilsen helpfully adds that "for many queer-identified youth, not 'coming out' can be a political statement, an act of resistance to notions of stable identity, and another way to underline the contextual nature of identity."[5] For a wide variety of reasons, LGBTQIA youth may determine that open self-disclosure of an LGBTQIA identity or inviting parents and family into the unfolding journey is simply not preferable at the moment. And that has to be a decision you honor and respect as a supportive presence they have invited into a sacred place in their lives.

In the discernment over whether or not to invite others in, there is also a concern about *how* to invite them in. Remember Patrick's question to Rev. Emilie: "Should I just sit down with my parents and have a conversation? I don't know if I want to see their reaction! Perhaps I should just write them a letter and get it all out first and then follow up with them later?" Teich identifies gossip and the Internet as two tools that can make coming out/inviting in easier and that can also make coming out/inviting in harder.[6] On the one hand, when LGBTQIA youth are trying to protect sacred places in their lives from those who would respond in rejecting or even violent ways, gossip and the Internet can be detrimental. On the other hand, when LGBTQIA youth decide they want the world to know, without having a thousand personal conversations about it, a post on social media can accomplish that quite easily. These "how" questions are important to consider with LGBTQIA youth, as there may be people in their lives—family members in particular—they would rather not find out through a social-media post before they've had the opportunity to invite them in more personally.

When and if LGBTQIA youth decide to invite family members into their sacred journeys, there are ways that you may be especially helpful to the youth and their families as a trusted pastor or lay ministry leader in your church or organization. Part of "inviting families in" is helping *all* family members develop respectful language about sexual and affectional orientation and gender identity. As the SAMHSA report referenced above suggests, "Many families and caregivers have not talked about these issues in a way that is not disparaging. For others, cultural silence about homosexuality is the norm, and talking about these issues may feel shameful and uncomfortable."[7] Whether it's breaking the family silence or helping to cultivate a new, respectful vocabulary, your knowledge and conversational presence with the family of LGBTQIA youth can become an invaluable resource.

COPING WITH INITIAL FAMILY REJECTION

Even when every indication says a family will respond positively to being invited in, family can surprise us. Other times, when rejection seems assured, family can still surprise us. But in any case, you should be prepared to help an LGBTQIA youth deal with the experience of family rejection. Experiencing a family in your congregation or community—people you know and love and respect—respond to their LGBTQIA youth with rejection can be painful and even shocking to witness. But your presence as their pastor, minister, or lay leader can be helpful to mitigate the harm caused by rejection between LGBTQIA youth and their families. But make no mistake about it: the potential harm is a serious concern.

Ryan and her colleagues found that, when compared to LGBT peers from families that reported no or low levels of family rejection, LGBT young adults who reported high levels of family rejection when they were adolescents were "8.4 times more likely to report having attempted suicide, 5.9 times more likely to report high levels of depression, 3.4 times more likely to use illegal drugs, and 3.4 times more likely to report having engaged in unprotected sexual intercourse."[8] Thus, family acceptance/rejection is critical—especially as the process of coming out/inviting in now regularly occurs at earlier and earlier ages.[9]

It is important to remember that many family members who perpetrate harmful or rejecting behavior toward their LGBTQIA children may see themselves as doing the best they can to "love" them.[10] Sometimes, even when they do really poorly, families may be doing the best they can in the moment. Your pastoral presence with LGBTQIA youth and their families can mean helping family members to see the ways that their words and actions may (even inadvertently) communicate rejection or enact harm, and to learn new ways of communicating love for their children.

At the same time, your pastoral presence with LGBTQIA youth may mean helping them to see the ways their family members are doing their best, helping them to see the possibility (though not the *guarantee*) that family members may gradually become more embracing of them. That being said, never lose sight of the fact that the LGBTQIA youth is in the vulnerable position in the family system—each youth's well-being must be your *primary* pastoral and ethical concern. Do not allow them to remain in situations in which abuse occurs or in which their physical health and well-being is put in jeopardy by the family's rejecting behavior. Greer adds,

> A youth minister should also plan ahead, creating a worst-case and best-case scenario to this meeting. Without having to share this plan with the youth or parents, a youth minister should have an idea of what they will do if the family totally rejects the teen. There is nothing worse than sitting in an office after parents leave abruptly and looking eye to teary eye with a very vulnerable, hurting teenager. As a minister, your emotions may also be running high and a clear plan of what options are available, what steps to take, what resources to utilize comes in very handy.[11]

You will find the section of the appendix related to family resources of use in helping you to think through such a plan of action and identify resources to utilize. I highly encourage you to think through that worksheet before a crisis need arises.

Don't give up hope, even when rejection is the *initial* reaction of parents and families to the disclosure or discovery of an LGBTQIA youth's identity. One study found that even families that initially reject their LGBTQIA youth become *less* rejecting over time. A critical factor in diminishing the level of rejection and helping parents and families learn to support their LGBTQIA children and youth is *access to accurate information*.[12] That's where you come in. As someone with a growing knowledge of sexual/affectional and gender identity, you can be an invaluable resource to families in your church and community. Depending on the geographical setting in which you live and work, you may be the *only* source of affirming and supportive knowledge to which a family has access. Please don't take this responsibility lightly!

In addition to the knowledge you may be able to share—gradually, and only when invited by the questions of youth and families—it would be helpful to build up a small library of resources to share, both print and online. When you recommend a book for a parent or youth to read, they may feel too embarrassed to go into a local bookstore and buy a book on LGBTQIA issues. Parents can just purchase these books online, but youth who don't have a credit or debit card may not have this option, and, even if they do, they may not feel comfortable having a book on LGBTQIA issues mailed to their homes, risking discovery by other family members. So have a few copies of your most helpful resources available to lend to youth and their families. In addition to books, organizations such as PFLAG produce helpful pamphlets on a variety of topics, and there are myriad online resources to explore. Be sure to explore these resources in advance so that you know you are recommending the best resources available to your youth and their families.

ADDRESSING CONFLICT BETWEEN PARENTS AND AMONG FAMILIES

Sometimes parents of an LGBTQIA teenager will not agree on how to address their child's gender identity or sexual/affectional orientation. At other times, conflict between parents and the LGBTQIA youth's other siblings may occur. Beyond the nuclear family, there may be conflicting perspectives on a youth's LGBTQIA identity among other family members. For example, an LGBTQIA youth may enjoy the gift of accepting parents and siblings but still have grandparents, aunts and uncles, or cousins with rejecting attitudes. Strain and stress on a marriage or within the family may arise if this is the case.

In your pastoral conversations with families, it may become clear to you that the skills required to intervene in the conflict are beyond your currently developed competency. In these cases, it can be helpful to know how to direct families to other supportive professionals. For example, knowing the difference between individual counseling and family therapy may help you make better referrals to youth and their families. There are certainly times at which an LGBTQIA youth may need the support of a therapist. But other times the LGBTQIA youth isn't necessarily the person who most "needs" the therapy. *The family* as a unit may be the best client for therapy. In these cases, a professional trained in family therapy may be the best option for referral. The family therapist will attend to the dynamics surrounding a youth's disclosure of LGBTQIA identity, and, hopefully, refrain from identifying the LGBTQIA youth as the focus of the therapy.

Having a list of a few licensed therapists—both individual and family therapists—who are competent in LGBTQIA concerns is invaluable when these needs arise. *Psychology Today* maintains a website that can be helpful in locating therapists in your city or region.[13] It includes an option to sort results based on those who work with gay and lesbian clients or those who address family conflict. But please, if you plan to refer a youth or family to a licensed therapist, be sure that you are responsible in your "ministry of introduction"; get to know the therapists you keep on your list so that you can be absolutely sure they are competent to address LGBTQIA concerns in an affirming manner. Most therapists are willing to speak to a potential referral source about their practice, so give them a call and get to know them first.

The SAMHSA report on helping families support their LGBT youth helpfully states that "the primary mechanism for change is helping families understand that there is a powerful relationship between their words, actions, and behaviors and their LGBT child's risk and well-being. Parental and caregiver reactions to an LGBT child or adolescent also affect their whole family."[14] When the conflict in question is between supportive and *affirming* parents and *non-affirming/rejecting* extended family members, your pastoral guidance in the midst of the crisis may be to help affirming parents understand the harm that can be caused to the LGBTQIA youth by the rejecting family members. At times, supportive parents will have to be firm with other family members who initially reject LGBTQIA youth, setting boundaries on what is acceptable speech and behavior about their child's sexual/affectional or gender identity, even refusing invitations to family events if these boundaries cannot be respected. This may feel harsh to some, but understanding the risks to emotional, spiritual, and physical well-being can help families see the importance of setting these boundaries.

HELPING SHIFT FAMILY NARRATIVES

The self-disclosure of an LGBTQIA identity to parents and family can sometimes create a sense of shock—though, at other times, parents have "known" at some intuitive level for some time. Parents may feel guilty that they somehow missed some signs of their child's gender identity or affectional orientation they "should have" noticed. That guilt may deepen if parents believe their teenager has experienced years of pain and turmoil without the support parents so desperately wish they could have provided.

Sometimes, denial, guilt, and expressions of grief may follow such a disclosure, whether it is brand new information or the confirmation of something intuitively known.[15] Other times, as Teich notes, "Parents may react with anger and hostility, feeling a combination of betrayal and a sense of loss."[16] Parents may temporarily place their own feelings before those of their LGBTQIA child, telling their youth they are being "selfish" and not considering the effects that their LGBTQIA identity may have on the family.[17] After the initial distress, however, parents often shift worries and concerns away from their child's identity as LGBTQIA and toward the implications of this identity; for example, the possible discrimination, rejection, abuse, or violence their child might face as an LGBTQIA person.[18]

In all of these cases, it is helpful to develop a sense of the kinds of stories being spun in the imaginations of parents and families and LGBTQIA youth leading up to the point of inviting parents in. In many instances, entire narratives that parents hold in their imaginations about how their child's life will play out have to be reworked considerably to take into account the disclosure of gender identity or affectional orientation.

Many parents may imagine a narrative of their child growing up and entering a heterosexual relationship, having children, and so on. This narrative is suddenly interrupted by the disclosure of a gay or lesbian identity. Or perhaps a trans youth self-disclosing gender identity to their parents suddenly halts the narrative flow the parents imagined of their child growing into adulthood as the gender assigned at birth. And while lesbian, gay, and trans identities are more and more visible in the wider world, what might it be like for parents whose youth discloses asexual identity? Asexuality is still so little understood and so underrepresented in popular culture that this disclosure represents a reality that is completely out of the realm of possibility for many parents to imagine—they simply have no frame of reference.

In coming to understand the stories parents and family members tell themselves about their children's lives, future stories are very important. Pay careful attention to what stories parents and youth are telling themselves about what the future may look like for the youth. An LGBTQIA youth's perception of what type of future is possible for them has implications for self-care practices, health promotion, decreasing risk-taking, and for developing career and personal aspirations.[19] As the SAMHSA report notes, "Many families who believe they are accepting are actually ambivalent about their child's sexual orientation and gender identity. Rather than expressing support, these families are instead giving their child mixed messages that contribute to health risks and diminished self-esteem."[20] Working with parents and families around the fears and sources of shame embedded in their imagined future for LGBTQIA youth can help in addressing these mixed messages.

For example, in the chapter vignette, Patrick's disclosure of his sexual identity came as a shock and temporarily halted his parents' ability to imagine a desirable future for their son. Their anger over that sense of loss clouded their ability to even think of what might be possible for Patrick. All they were able to think about in the days following Patrick's disclosure was that Patrick, their only child, would never fall in love with and marry a woman or have grandchildren for them in the way they imagined. They were consumed by how much of a loss that felt like to them.

Rev. Emilie's question to Brian and Allison—"I wonder if you can imagine what life might be like for Patrick if he meets a *man* with whom he falls in love"—is a helpful example of a question that provokes the imagination back to life when it has been temporarily halted by shock or grief over losing a previously held future narrative. Or a question about the *qualities* they imagine in their child's future spouse or partner can move parents away from a gendered picture to focus on the qualities of love and support and respect they hope their child will find in a partner. All of these qualities of relationship are possible for their child to find, regardless of the gender of the spouse or partner. Such simple questions may help parents see a future that was previously unimaginable. The social or religious stories that surround them, about what it looks like to fall in love or get married or build a family, have never *invited* them to imagine such possibilities. As in Patrick's case, even the prospect of family members moving from a rejecting attitude to a more "neutral"—though not yet fully *accepting*—attitude can have positive effects on the health and well-being of their LGBTQIA youth.

It can also be helpful to ask yourself how *religious narratives and beliefs* shape parents' hopes and dreams and imagined futures for their LGBTQIA children. Religious narratives about relationships and family and sex are so strong—drawing upon symbols of the sacred to give them legitimacy—that they can be a challenge to rework. This may require some careful biblical and theological conversation about where these assumptions come from, as well as offering alternative perspectives on the interpretation of Scripture or the theological perspectives parents have adopted, perhaps without ever thinking them through. Getting some clarity about how these narratives inform parents' perspectives about their child's LGBTQIA identity may help you identify potential ways forward. Naming where narratives no longer fit their child's future can give way to new possibilities for a preferred future of health, well-being, and fulfillment.[21]

HELPING YOUTH HURT BY FAMILY MEMBERS

Sometimes, in the midst of the shock or anger or grief that parents and families feel after the disclosure of LGBTQIA identities, they behave in ways that cause pain to their LGBTQIA child. This may necessitate attempts at repairing the relational damage done by the negative reactions of family members. Pastoral and ministerial leaders are uniquely suited for this role, as they often serve in an institutional setting where both the youth and family members are active participants. I will note at the outset of this discussion: If the harm rises to the level of physical abuse, it should be reported to the appropriate authorities in your city or county. As of 2023, twenty-nine states include clergy among the professionals mandated by law to report child abuse; and in sixteen states, *anyone* who suspects such abuse is required to report it.[22] Whether or not the law mandates reporting, the ethic of standing in solidarity with those most vulnerable to harm compels us to take appropriate actions to preserve the safety and well-being of LGBTQIA youth in abusive situations.

Aside from outright abuse, there are many instances in which an LGBTQIA youth may experience emotional or spiritual harm from the actions of a parent or family member. These instances are the focus of this section. Both fully accepting family members and those currently rejecting but on the journey to becoming accepting may behave in ways that cause pain to LGBTQIA youth. Some examples you may encounter include:

—LGBTQIA youth being blamed for the bullying, rejection, and abuse they suffer at school or other arenas as a result of their LGBTQIA identity.

—Being pressured by family members to try to "change" their sexual orientation or gender identity.
—Being punished and even, at times, abused verbally, physically, or spiritually for claiming their LGBTQIA identity.
—Being kicked out of the home for any period of time as a punishment for an LGBTQIA identity.
—Using religious messages to shame an LGBTQIA youth or justify punishment.
—Parents and family rejecting their child's LGBTQIA friends or significant others in the home because of their affectional orientation or gender identity.
—Parents refusing to allow the teenager to dress in a way that reflects the teen's gender identity and expression.

Responding to the needs that arise in the life of an LGBTQIA youth when something like expulsion from the home or bullying at school occurs is covered in chapter 3. But responding to the *lingering hurt and pain* that youth experience when these things happen needs a bit of extra attention in at least two areas.

First, the situations of familial hurt that arise in the life of an LGBTQIA youth may prompt discussions about how to *set boundaries* with family members who are both rejecting and insistent upon behavior that perpetuates emotional and spiritual harm to the youth. This could take many forms, but one example is the boundary that Rev. Emilie helped Brian set in relation to his son, Patrick. When Brian's negative views of his son's sexuality became the topic of every conversation at dinner and on family outings, it hindered their ability to even be together as a family. So Brian agreed to cease this type of conversation for the time being, knowing that Patrick had heard him express his perspectives many times now, thus freeing up their conversational space to include other topics, since they both want to have a relationship despite Brian's reservations about his son's affectional orientation.

Second, it may help to engage in pastoral conversation with youth about what it means to *forgive parents and family members* who have hurt them in relation to their LGBTQIA identities. It is important to note that pressuring youth, or any victim-survivor of abuse, to forgive their abuser is itself a spiritually abusive practice. Any conversations about what forgiveness might mean in these situations should come from the victim-survivor of abuse and great care should be taken to understand what the person means by "forgiveness" and what that forgiveness might mean to them. For example, for some it is a practice of letting go of the anger they hold toward abusers but does not proceed to relational reconciliation with the abuser.

Here, I would suggest your conversation help youth to understand the differences between "forgiving" and "forgetting"—the former doesn't necessitate the latter—and between forgiveness and continuing to put oneself in positions where harm is likely to occur.

In the first instance, it is important for those harmed by family members to know that enacting forgiveness doesn't mean forgetting the harm caused, which could very well be an impossible task anyway. Even in the midst of forgiveness, the victim recognizes the wrong that was done and the harm it has caused to one's psyche, soul, and relationships. Forgiveness is the relational stance that says, "I won't hold your wrongdoing against you forever." For LGBTQIA children who wish to have relationships with their parents—even *rejecting* parents—this may be a desirable relational stance, especially when they are no longer in the position of being submitted to continued harm (e.g., when they are no longer dependent on their parents or have moved out of the house).

In the second instance, forgiveness never requires one to continue to put oneself in positions where harm is likely to occur. Too much harm and abuse is perpetrated when biblical notions of forgiveness are distorted to mean that harm and abuse simply have to be endured. Whatever directions your discussions about forgiveness take, they should *always* be guided by the LGBTQIA youth's desires related to relationships with parents and family. Forgiveness should never be forced on a youth as a necessary next step in family relationships.

CREATING SUPPORTIVE COMMUNITIES FOR PARENTS AND FAMILIES

It is likely that many parents of LGBTQIA youth have no other adult peers with whom they can talk about their experience of having an LGBTQIA child. This feeling of isolation from a formerly understanding, empathic community may be exacerbated if most of the parent's friendships are with others in conservative religious circles that are not affirming of LGBTQIA identities. From non-LGBTQIA-affirming friends, parents of LGBTQIA teenagers may experience blaming and shaming from their adult peers who see their child's sexual or gender identity as the parents' "fault" and evidence of "sin" in their child's life. Even for parents who are theologically resolved to support and affirm their LGBTQIA youth, the lack of peers who understand and support this stance can be discouraging, to say the least.

One of the most helpful, and historic, community resources supporting the family and friends of LGBTQ+ youth is PFLAG. Their website is full of helpful and accessible resources for the family of LGBTQ+ youth as well as a link to locate a local PFLAG chapter and meeting in your area of the country.[23] At a PFLAG meeting, educational presentations are often given, alongside ample time for personal sharing and reflection among the families, friends, and LGBTQ+ people who attend. I encourage you to visit one of these meetings so that you will know what you are recommending, should you ever believe this to be a helpful resource to the families of your LGBTQ+ youth.

Research shows that contact with other parents who have LGBTQIA children is helpful in working through distress and correcting false assumptions parents make about LGBTQIA people.[24] If you don't know whether or not your community has a local PFLAG chapter, go to your computer right now, access https://www.pflag.org, and search their chapter network for a local chapter. If you find a meeting, write down the pertinent information in your address book or smartphone so that it's easily accessible. This may be invaluable information for your youth or their parents at some point. If there is no local PFLAG chapter that is easily accessible to your youth and families, gather a few supportive people, educate them about PFLAG, and consider what it would take to start a chapter in your area. Alternately, there are online forums where parents can engage more anonymously in conversation with other parents of LGBTQIA kids for mutual support. I encourage you to vet any sites you find thoroughly before passing them along to parents.

INVITING *NEW* FAMILY MEMBERS IN

There's one other important dimension to inviting family in that I want to raise here. In addition to the conversations surrounding how to invite parents and family into an LGBTQIA youth's unfolding sense of sexual/affectional and gender identity, many LGBTQIA people need to invite *new* family members into their lives beyond the dictates of biology—a "chosen family." Julie Tilsen rightly notes, "Unlike other marginalized groups, where youth share the same social locations as their parents and other family and community members, queer youth are likely to be alone in their queerness with their family. . . . Sadly, it is often in these contexts, where other young people gain support and protection, that queer youth experience violence to their psyches and their bodies."[25]

As "host" to their own sacred life spaces, LGBTQIA youth may decide to "invite in" other supportive adults, their LGBTQIA peers, and supportive leaders in their congregation to places of familial intimacy, especially at times when one's given family can't meet all of the emotional, relational, and spiritual needs that many typically receive from biological or legally adoptive families. Yet many LGBTQIA youth may hesitate to invite others into these places of familial intimacy, and, therefore, go without necessary support and resources long after experiencing family rejection. Avery Belyeu, a survivor of family rejection who has long worked as a professional in suicide prevention with LGBTQIA youth, says,

> A common feeling among queer youth who are survivors of family rejection is a sense of being a burden. This concern and worry about being a burden will likely prevent many queer youth who are experiencing family rejection from just inviting people in as new surrogate family. The thoughts they might have may include: "Well, I don't want to be a bother," and even, "What if they don't want me around either?" Post family rejection, many queer youth will have a heightened since of vigilance about potential rejection from others and will avoid it at all cost. This is why it is essential that the burden of building and being that family must rest *not* with the queer youth but with other adults who recognize this is needed.[26]

Belyeu rightly says, "I think that the role of the youth minister may be to think about how to facilitate the process of assisting loving and caring adults in their congregation to proactively reach out and be the family of choice needed by the LGBTQIA survivor of family rejection."[27]

This need for "new" chosen family members may be due to lack of support from biological or adoptive family; but chosen family may also fill places in an LGBTQIA youth's life that even the most supportive and embracing family can't fulfill—for example, LGBTQIA peers and LGBTQIA adult mentors in a family in which the youth is the only LGBTQIA-identified person. For whatever reason the need arises, Belyeu notes the simple but profoundly important roles "chosen family" can play in the lives of LGBTQIA youth,

When an LGBTQIA young person is rejected by their family, they need adults who can assess this reality and find ways to show up for the youth. For instance inviting the youth to come over for a family dinner. Inviting them to join on day-to-day mundane outings (not just special occasions). Checking in on them spontaneously on the phone, via text, etc., to see how they are. Gently asking questions about how they can be of help with finances if that is realistic.[28]

As a youth ministry leader, you may be in the best position in your youth's community constellation to aid them in figuring out who these supportive adults might be, and then facilitating the establishment of a caring and supportive relationship that may be, quite literally, life saving and will be, at the very least, profoundly life-*giving* to everyone involved.

A NOTE TO PARENTS OF LGBTQIA YOUTH

I am hopeful that some readers of this book are parents of LGBTQIA youth. You, too, may need sources of support and guidance as you come to understand your child's developing sense of LGBTQIA identity. You need folks who will listen deeply to you, hold your story as sacred, and nonjudgmentally explore with you the many factors—including the theological and spiritual—that shape your perspectives on parenting LGBTQIA youth. Having this support may help you to address your personal reactions to your LGBTQIA child's identity in ways that provide space for you to vent and process with supportive peers while, at the same time, meeting your child's need for a parent to provide the love, safety, and support that every kid needs.[29]

At times, the reworking of your family narratives will mean finding ways to work through the disappointment, or even shame, at discovering that you are among the *last people* in your child's life to be invited in to the awareness of an LGBTQIA identity. While it is understandable that this reality may temporarily shatter former perceptions of familial closeness, I hope you can understand the risk that it is for your child to invite you in, simply because the stakes are so high and your child's relationship with you is so important. I hope you can come to feel honored that you were invited in when you were and that you can be a supportive companion on the journey.

Adjustment periods to newly disclosed affectional and gender identities are normal for parents and family members, so give yourself some time. But even in the midst of what may feel like a lot of uncertainty about being invited in to this part of your child's journey, I am hopeful that you will find ways to offer the unconditional love, care, and support that your LGBTQIA child needs from you. This will go a lot further toward supporting his or her or their well-being into the future than anything else you can do—research attests to it and, most likely, your parental intuition does, too.

If all of your reading and talking with others and exploring your questions still has you wondering if you can embrace your child's LGBTQIA identity, I offer you this final encouragement: pray for your child. Don't use too many words or pray for your desired "outcomes." Just pray simply for your child's health and well-being and fulfillment in life and for God's grace and guidance on the journey. If you can't quite form words without your own notions about gender and sexual identity coming out, then just bring an image of your child to mind. Picture your child being held in the light of God's love, and let that image linger prayerfully in your mind's eye for a while. In this way, you invite the Spirit to work in your heart and mind in ways that may be surprising.[30]

5
A Brief Guide to Pastoral and Mentoring Relationships with LGBTQIA Youth

Trina is fourteen years old and a member of Harborview Church. Over the past couple of years, she has become close to Tim, one of the laypeople who volunteer with the youth group at Harborview. In his late fifties, Tim experiences his work with the youth of Harborview as both a challenging and meaningful ministry and never misses an opportunity to chaperone a trip or lead a Bible study. Tim has been teaching the Sunday school class that Trina attends for the past two years and always finds Trina's input in the class insightful and spiritually mature.

Trina and Tim have shared many deep and personal conversations about Trina's life and faith and future, on various youth trips and over coffee on Sunday mornings before Sunday school. Trina is trans—many at the church have known her since birth and have witnessed her gradual transition over the past three years. Many of the conversations between Trina and Tim address some of the issues that have arisen over the course of her transition the past couple of years. Trina is fortunate to have parents who are committed to Trina living into the fullness of her being, embracing her gender identity, and helping her to transition at the speed that Trina determines is best for her.

Tim has been one of her fiercest companions in her process of inviting the congregation to join her on the journey of her emerging identity as a young trans woman. He's always been the one to help the other youth when they struggle to make the switch from her name given at birth to "Trina" when she began regularly presenting as a woman. When Trina first began her transition, Tim even held a dinner and information session in his home for several of the other youth ministry volunteers and the ministerial staff of the church to which he invited a trans man and educator from the nearby LGBTQ center to speak to the group about gender identity and the needs of trans people in the earliest stages of transition. Tim knew that no matter how supportive Trina's parents are, this would be brand new territory for most of the people at Harborview Church, and having an informed group of ministry leaders would help cultivate the most welcoming and affirming community of faith possible for Trina.

Trina asks Tim if they can meet for coffee at the donut shop across the street from church before Sunday school and Tim gladly agrees. It's June, and Trina is going to be a freshman in high school this fall. She shares with Tim that she is getting nervous about going to high school with a lot of new kids who don't know her or her story.

Tim invites Trina to talk a little about her concerns, "Going to a new school is usually a little nerve-racking for a lot of people. Tell me something about how you're imagining this move. What are you most looking forward to? What are you concerned about?"

Trina shares with Tim, saying, "Well, I'm super excited about starting marching band at the high school. They have an amazing reputation, and I can't wait to be a part of something like that. I'm really excited about more challenging classes that are going to prepare me for college and help me explore what I might want to do when I grow up. But Mom and Dad are worried about me going to a new school with so many new students and teachers who don't know my story. I think they're worried I'll be bullied or something. I think they'd rather me to go a smaller private school, but that would rule out marching band."

"I see," Tim says. "It seems like your parents are worried about how safe you'll be with your new classmates and teachers—whether they'll be as supportive to you as your

middle school has been. But what about you? Is that your concern or just your parents' worry?"

"Well, I'm not that concerned about it, really. I know I may be picked on and singled out and misunderstood. I don't like it, but I've figured out ways of dealing with it. And I know the school already has a gay-straight alliance that I'm sure will be a good source of support. So, no, I guess I'm not that concerned about it. I've been getting nervous hearing my parents talk about it, but I think I'll be fine."

Tim says to Trina, "It sounds like you've really thought about this and have a realistic perspective on what the challenges of a new school might be. You seem to feel confident that you can handle those challenges and use the resources available to you there."

"Yeah, I guess that's right. I just needed to say it out loud to figure out what I really felt about moving to a new school," Trina says. "Thanks for listening, Tim."

"Trina, I'm really inspired by how confident you are in living out your sense of call to embody the gender that God created you to be," Tim says. "I'm curious after these couple of years in transition, how your spirituality deepened through the process. What are you learning from this experience about God and what it means to follow God's call on your life?"

Tim and Trina talked for the next hour and nearly missed Sunday school.

MENTORING LGBTQIA TEENS AS A STRAIGHT/CISGENDER ADULT

In writing this book, I imagined that many readers would be straight and cisgender ministers and lay leaders seeking to develop their competency in addressing the needs of LGBTQIA youth. If this describes you, then you may sometimes wonder if you can best meet the pastoral and mentoring needs of LGBTQIA youth as a cisgender and straight person. The short answer is: Absolutely you can!

Of course, it is important for LGBTQIA youth to experience LGBTQIA adults in leadership positions—as ministers, teachers, coaches, and so on—as well as to see LGBTQIA people visible in society. But please do not underestimate the importance of straight and cisgender people as supportive and affirming mentors on the journey. When you are a cisgender or straight person in *religious* leadership, the significance of that affirming presence is enhanced even more, as churches have long been difficult places for LGBTQIA people to find support.

On a personal note, when I began inviting others into my own sacred journey—at a time when both my sense of vocational call to ministry and the living out of my affectional orientation in relationship with another man were merging—almost every supportive presence I had in the earliest days were straight and cisgender people: ministers from my church, friends, seminary professors, and so on. The ways they became appreciative allies to me on my journey created space for me to explore these intersecting realities in my life and more fully live into my sense of who the Divine was calling me to become. If it hadn't been for these straight and cisgender pastors and mentors and friends, my journey would have been a very lonely one. Please don't underestimate your importance as a straight or cisgender pastoral or mentoring presence.

I also assumed in writing this book that some readers serve in churches that are not necessarily affirming of LGBTQIA people. This may mean that your pastoral and mentoring support of LGBTQIA youth is complicated by the need to address larger congregational dynamics that may be quite negative toward LGBTQIA people or, at the very least, silencing of overt attempts to express positive messages to and about LGBTQIA people. This makes your presence in the congregation as a supportive and affirming adult presence all the more important, especially when many youth don't necessarily have the choice of where or whether to attend church, but come with parents or other family members. By now, I hope you are convinced that your role as a straight, cisgender ministry leader is vital to the health and well-being of the youth in your congregation!

ASKING QUESTIONS AND INVITING STORIES

The LGBTQIA youth who come to you for care aren't coming to you for all of the answers. They are coming to know you and to be known by you as a caring and supportive presence in their lives—this means listening compassionately and attentively to the stories of your

LGBTQIA youth. Pastoral theologian Carrie Doehring describes the importance of hearing stories in providing pastoral care:

> Stories allow people to lament with each other—express anger and question all they know about life—without imposing meanings prematurely. In the process of telling stories, people become authors, instinctively finding a story's beginning and climax and imagining various endings. When pastoral care is experienced as narrative it becomes more relational and communal.[1]

As a pastoral or mentoring presence, it is important for you to *ask good questions*, inviting rich story to emerge in the conversation.

Tilsen helps those who work with LGBTQIA youth to consider how to draw out the "storied embodiment" of a youth's experience of sexual and gender identity. "Be sure to invite stories—not simply 'facts'—so that people's accounts of themselves are rich, situated, and contextualized. . . . Ask about meanings, reflections, preferences, and hopes; this encourages stories that can be told with dignity and heard with respect."[2] When you begin formulating a question in conversation, ask yourself: Does this question invite story or simple facts? Can it be addressed with a yes or no response, or does it invite youth to talk about meanings they are making about life and reflections on their experience and hopes for their future? Unless you are really looking for "just the facts" about something, opt for questions that will help youth tell their stories, like Tim does in the chapter vignette.

For example, when a problem arises in an LGBTQIA youth's life, it is important to get clear about what exactly that problem is and for whom. "What's the problem and for whom?" is a question you might hold in the back of your mind as you first begin hearing the problem story. The parent of an LGBTQIA youth may see the "problem" as their child's LGBTQIA identity, perhaps even identifying the problem as their child's "choice" to be LGBTQIA. The *youth*, however, may not see LGBTQIA identity as a "problem" at all. Instead the youth may locate the problem in family rejection of the youth as an LGBTQIA person, or a school environment hostile to LGBTQIA students, or to unresolved conflicts and questions between the person's LGBTQIA identity and religious faith. As narrative therapists say: the *person* is never the problem, the *problem* is the problem. Especially when LGBTQIA people are so often identified as "problems" by families and churches, it is vital that you come to know how the LGBTQIA youth sees the issues and their impact on the youth's well-being, rather than taking at face value the ways other people in the youth's life are telling the problem story.

Note how Tim gets at this in the chapter vignette with the simple question, "It seems like your parents are worried about how safe you'll be with your new classmates and teachers—whether they'll be as supportive to you as your middle school has been. But what about you? Is that your concern or just your parents' worry?" With this question, Tim discovers with Trina that she actually feels quite resourceful to meet the challenges of a new school and has simply been taking on a lot of her parent's anxiety that isn't really her own. He invites a story of Trina's competency and ability related to a potentially difficult move to a new school in the midst of her own gender transition. Asking good, open, curious questions can help youth feel more comfortable getting into some of the areas of conversation they are hesitant to bring up in the early stages of dialogue but that they really wish to discuss with you as a pastoral or mentoring figure.

TALKING ABOUT SEX WITH LGBTQIA TEENS

It should come as no surprise that when working with LGBTQIA youth—or any youth, for that matter—the topic of sex may arise. While many youth are exposed to sexuality education in their school's curriculum, there is often no education whatsoever on same-sex sexuality or on gender identity and expression. There are several states with laws prohibiting public school teachers from even *talking* about the reality of lesbian, gay, bisexual, and transgender people in the classroom.[3] So even if your LGBTQIA youth experience a sexuality education program in school, it may not include their lived experience. In many instances, parents will not be go-to sources of information on sexuality for LGBTQIA youth either. If you are an adult with whom an LGBTQIA youth has entered into a trusting, affirming pastoral or mentoring relationship, you may be one of the few non-Internet sources for exploring questions related to sex.

It is understandable if you don't feel entirely up to being a repository of information on sex, sexuality, and gender identity and expression. In fact, in all of the exposure you've had to sexuality education, you may not have encountered LGBTQIA topics covered either. If that's the case, you need to do your homework in order to be a more helpful pastoral presence to youth exploring these questions. Two websites that can be helpful for accessing resources for both your own education and that of your youth are the Sexuality Information and Education Council of the United States[4] and Advocates for Youth.[5]

A few questions that LGBTQIA activist Sue Hyde poses that are helpful starting places for reflection about the kinds of questions youth may bring to you for conversation are these:

—"What were some of our first sexual experiences and what did we learn from those? . . .
—What kind of sexual activities best express who we are and what we want and like? . . .
—How does our own understanding of masculinity, femininity, and gender variance affect how we think about LGBT sexuality and community? . . .
—If sex is not in the context of a long-term relationship, is it OK? What constitutes immoral or unacceptable sex and sexuality?"[6]

Note the ways that these questions invite reflection and meaning making, rather than too quickly determining the "right" answer. This may feel a bit uncomfortable to you if your religious tradition establishes strict ways of thinking about such questions. But, as Doehring suggests, "Narratives illustrate the ways that people embody values and beliefs in daily practices," and questions like the above help you to enter into a process of discernment with LGBTQIA youth about questions of sex that draw out, in story, the ways their religious beliefs are embodied in their lives, not just held in their heads.[7]

It is also important to consider what biases and assumptions you bring into a conversation with an LGBTQIA youth so that those don't get in the way of youth telling their own stories and making meaning in conversation with you, rather than you imposing *your* meaning onto them. Carefully consider your own assumptions and biases about LGBTQIA sexuality and where these assumptions come from so that, when they arise in your mind during pastoral conversation, you can check yourself before imposing your system of values and meaning making onto youth, rather than helping them to do that work in conversation *with* you.

Beyond preparing yourself for the role of helping youth navigate their questions concerning sex and sexuality, you may also be in a position to consider whether your congregation is ready to offer a spiritually integrated sexuality education program, if you don't do so already. One such program that is widely used in mainline denominations is called *Our Whole Lives*, published by the Unitarian Universalist Association and the United Church of Christ, and it includes curriculum appropriate for ages across the lifespan.

REFLECTING THEOLOGICALLY WITH LGBTQIA TEENS

Besides sex, the other topic that you should expect to address with LGBTQIA youth who seek you out for care and mentoring are questions about God, religion, and spirituality. Never underestimate the connection of our sexual/affectional and gender identities to our experience of the Divine and practice of religion and spirituality. James Nelson helped a generation of theologians turn their theological attention from "above" toward our bodies and what they have to teach us about God. Nelson called this "body theology," which he says, "is nothing more, nothing less than our attempts to reflect on body experience as revelatory of God."[8] This reorientation toward religious questions significantly shifts our attention from questions like, "What do our religious beliefs say about x, y, or z?" to what our bodies and experiences of sexuality and gender identity are teaching us about God. James Nickoloff poignantly adds,

> Those who consider either faith or sex in isolation from (or even worse, in opposition to) the other inevitably fail to plumb the depths of both. Can sexuality legitimately be conceived apart from its spiritual meaning, its mystery? Can the life of faith adequately be understood apart from a consideration of the most intimate and potentially humanizing dimensions of our lives?[9]

In pastoral and mentoring relationships, paying attention to the meaning LGBTQIA youth are making of their sexual and gender identities is an important pastoral act. And this meaning making is never a solitary process. The voices of parents and pastors and the media and snippets of things youth have read and conversations they've overheard all become part of the narrative material out of which they begin telling their own stories of meaning in relation to sexual and gender experience. As addressed in chapter 3, many of the religious messages LGBTQIA youth receive contribute to a type of precariousness of the soul that can grow to make life seem unlivable.

Nelson says that in the way we intentionally engage in exploration of the connection of our bodies with our understanding and approach to God, we need to ask, "How can we understand both the givenness of our body realities and the meaning that we ascribe to them, and how can we interpret these in ways that nurture the greater wholeness of our lives in relation to God, each other, and the earth?"[10] If youth are making meaning of their sexuality or gender identity in theological ways that do not lead to greater wholeness and help nurture health and well-being, conversation with a pastoral or mentoring figure may help to rework some of these harmful narratives so that life can be lived in greater fullness.

This may mean developing a *queer eye* toward theology. In this sense, I am using *queer*, not as a marker of identity, but as an activity (a *queering*) in relation to meaning making. Tilsen says, "To *queer* something is an emergent process of disrupting expected norms in such a way that new possibilities emerge and standard, unquestioned practices become open for interrogation."[11] Even the simple shift from a question like, "What does God say about my sexuality or gender identity?" to a question like, "What does my embodiment of sexuality or gender identity have to teach me about God?" invites a queering conversation. Inviting LGBTQIA youth to become authorities on their own experience and to make religious meaning out of that experience is a significant queer movement in a cultural landscape in which religious authorities have always purported to be the ultimate authority on LGBTQIA people's lives.

Even the experiences of rejection and isolation can be the starting place for exploration into one's own religious or spiritual meaning making. As Nickoloff says, "Not 'fitting in' can be a step on the road to a healthy self-affirmation and, ultimately, a step on the road to God, as the mystical traditions of many religions teach us."[12] Those who are deemed outsiders to the religious establishment often hold special potential in teaching us who we are as human beings and our relationship to God. Invite youth to move from being the *subject* of other's stories about them to *authors* of their own stories. Making meaning of their own experience in conversation with an appreciative pastoral ally like you can feel life-giving and liberating. This is what Tim does in the chapter vignette when he asks, "I'm curious after these couple of years in transition, how has your spirituality deepened through the process? What are you learning about God and what it means to follow God's call on your life?"

In these pastoral and mentoring conversations with LGBTQIA youth, you are creating space and expanding the potential for youth to become authors in their own storytelling, meaning-making explorations. In this way, you are engaging in an important pastoral act of expanding the "recognizability" of LGBTQIA youth. Judith Butler says,

> [I]f we cannot find our way within the norms of gender or sexuality assigned to us, or can only find our way with great difficulty, we are exposed to what it means to be at the limits of recognizability: this situation can be, depending on the circumstance, both terrible and exhilarating. To exist at such a limit means that the very viability of one's life is called into question. . . . It also means that we can be at the threshold of developing the terms that allow us to live.[13]

When you offer a space of compassion and affirmation, treat youth as the authorities on their own experience—as competent to explore ultimate questions about God and spirituality—and invite the sacredness of their stories into pastoral conversation, then you are expanding the potential for them to develop the terms that allow them to live into health, well-being, and spiritual vitality. Your empathetic, pastoral presence may be one of the first relational spaces in which LGBTQIA youth are able to live outside of the norms and terms of assigned gender or sexuality norms and terms that may not fit their lived experience and that may have called the viability of their lives into question.

If you are invited into this journey alongside an LGBTQIA youth then, friends, consider yourself blessed. It may be difficult and, at times, fraught with conflict and anxiety, filled with questions you have never considered, and even with feelings of inadequacy as a pastoral or mentoring presence. But it is a sacred calling; and the gift that you have to offer is your affirming, supportive, and gracious presence, through which some LGBTQIA youth may come to more fully know the loving presence of the Divine. Blessings on the journey.

6
A Brief Guide to Queer Neurodiversity

Jordan began volunteering as a youth group leader at her small-town Lutheran church a few years ago, loving the opportunity to spend Wednesday evenings with the church's small group of teens. After about a year of working with the group, the church council asked if Jordan would step into the role of youth director. She gladly accepted!

Jordan loved embodying the church's commitment to LGBTQIA affirmation in the youth ministry—the only affirming youth group within about a forty-mile radius. The ten to twelve regulars in the group would often invite their LGBTQIA friends from school to youth group events, and it was one of Jordan's favorite experiences to see these new teens finding a place of unconditional embrace among the other youth and adult volunteers. One of the visiting youth once told her that the youth group was the first place they felt like they didn't have to hide and could be fully themselves.

As the youth group grew bit by bit, Jordan started to notice that there were times when it was hard to get through the planned activity, lesson, and prayer time that was their usual rhythm on Wednesdays. A few of the youth seemed restless and distracted pretty early into the evening. Another regular seemed withdrawn from the others, which worried

Jordan that this youth was not feeling included. Occasionally, no matter how many times Jordan gave verbal instructions about an activity, there were a few who just never seemed to understand the activity.

Frustrated and a bit discouraged for the first time in her experience working with the youth, Jordan reached out to her friend in the congregation, Dawn, who is a middle school English teacher. Over coffee, Jordan told Dawn about the experience and asked for advice. Dawn listened and validated that it seemed to be a really frustrating experience for Jordan. Then Dawn offered that it sounded similar to her own experience early on with some of her first students who were neurodivergent, often coming into the classroom with notes from parents or doctors or with individual accommodation plans (IAPs) from the district psychologist. It was a process of learning and peer-to-peer consultation for Dawn, but she began developing ways of better supporting these students in their learning in the classroom. And Dawn offered to talk periodically with Jordan about some of what she learned over time.

Through these conversations, Jordan started to realize that there were a lot of unwritten rules about how the youth group operated: The youth group was always an hour. The activities were always highly interpersonal and high energy. Afterward, the youth were expected to come down from that high and sit for the rest of the time for Bible study, which was very discussion oriented. Prayer at the end was assumed to be quiet and verbal.

Jordan recognized that for some youth with ADHD or autism or any number of neurodivergent bodyminds, these unwritten rules just weren't working because they weren't designed with these youth in mind. She started experimenting with other formats for Wednesday evenings: She cut the evening activities down to forty-five minutes, which seemed more manageable for many youth. And those who wanted to linger afterward could. They began alternating between more high-energy activities some weeks, like games that required a lot of body movement and interaction, and quieter and more reflective activities other weeks, like art projects that didn't require much interaction. Bible study became less of a sit-still-and-discuss pro-

cess and incorporated visual elements, movement, and ways of keeping the body engaged for those who concentrated better that way. She stopped worrying so much when some youth seemed to withdraw a little from the group and even began accommodating that need in the way she arranged the space in the youth room, with some chairs further apart from others. And one thing she learned from Dawn that she incorporated immediately was to provide both written and verbal instructions anytime they were necessary, which was a game changer.

A few months into some of Jordan's changed approaches to the youth group's time, one of the newer members of the group came to Jordan and said, "I know a lot of the queer and trans people in the youth group really appreciate Wednesday nights here as a place where we can unmask and be ourselves. But I wanted you to know that this is one of the only places where I feel like I can let my neurospicy self shine, too, without anyone expecting me to fit into boxes that don't work for me."[1] *Jordan knew she was in the right place.*

THE LANGUAGE OF NEURODIVERSITY

One of the gifts of our human differences are the ways our bodies and minds work. To better represent the holistic nature of body and mind, I'll use the term *bodymind* in this chapter. Neurodiversity is a gift to our communities of faith and a feature of the Divine's pluriform creation. This chapter aims to help you begin developing a *neuroinclusive*, LGBTQIA-affirming youth ministry. While there is no absolute overlap between sexual and gender diversity and neurodivergence, there are significant enough intersections between neurodivergent people and LGBTQIA people that it is an important area for inclusive youth ministry leaders to be versed in.

First, a few definitions are helpful for those unfamiliar with the terminology: *Neurodiversity* simply describes the fact of our holistic bodyminds and the ways they work differently from person to person. We're all part of a neurodiverse world, just like we're all part of a world of gender diversity and sexual diversity, whether we're straight, cis, or LGBTQIA.

The term *neurodivergent* describes those whose bodymind functions differently from the majority of people. We most often think of autism as a form of neurodivergence. But many would also place other ways in which our bodyminds differ from one another in the category of neurodivergence, such as ADHD, dyslexia, OCD, and mental health concerns like depression or bipolar. United Church of Christ minister Sarah Griffith Lund says, "To label oneself as neurodivergent means one intentionally includes oneself in the community of people whose brains are part of the diversity of human expression. . . . To be neurodivergent is an identity that celebrates one's brain difference as contributing to humankind rather than being a deficit."[2]

Neurotypical describes people who "live, act, and experience the world in a way that consistently falls within the boundaries of neuronormativity—that is, within the boundaries of what the prevailing culture *imagines* a person with a 'normal mind' to be like."[3] The key word in this definition is *imagines*. Our dominant cultures, the structures of our everyday lives, the ways we talk about and accommodate differences *assumes* that there is a "right" or "normal" or "healthy" way of being for our bodyminds. But as a matter of diversity (*not pathology*), neurodiversity is simply a matter of fact in our lives. Most communities, however, are arranged with neurotypical people in mind–a reality that a *neuro-informed* and *neuroinclusive* community aims to correct.

Try to internalize the reality that there is no normal, just many ways of being, some of which are accommodated far better by our society than others, meaning that some people are disabled by society's lack of accommodation of their particular bodymind. Nick Walker, contributor to the development of the neurodiversity paradigm and neuroqueer theory, helpfully points out that "the precise degree to which you're disabled depends on how well your access needs are accommodated."[4] Our role in cultivating neuroinclusive ministries is to enable people with neurodivergent bodyminds to flourish rather than contribute to their disablement through our lack of concern for their access needs and bodymind differences.

LGBTQIA AND NEURODIVERGENT INTERSECTIONS

Anyone who has cultivated an intentionally LGBTQIA-inclusive space for youth has likely noticed that neurodivergent youth are showing up, too—sometimes they are also LGBTQIA and sometimes not. One reason is simply that spaces that are cultivated with an intentional ethic of inclusivity, belonging, and deep care attract many people who have often experienced exclusion, marginalization, and bullying or violence in other settings—queer, trans, and neurodivergent youth along with youth who have simply not found a warm embrace among their peers in other spaces. But there may also be a statistical reality behind this convergence too.

For example, autistic people are statistically more likely than neurotypical people to be LGBTQ+.[5] For a long time, we wrongly assumed that autistic people overall were not interested in sexual or romantic relationships. This occurs because of both heterosexist assumptions about sexuality and misunderstandings about neurodivergent sexual and romantic orientations, though it is also statistically the case that autistic adolescents and adults are about eight times more likely to identify as asexual than their neurotypical peers.[6] Additionally, trans and gender-diverse people who do not identify with the sex they were assigned at birth are six times as likely to be diagnosed as autistic than their cisgender peers.[7] While we do not yet know why this may be, one theory is that neurodivergent people tend to be less beholden to the social norms of binary gender. Yet prejudice also leads to care providers mistakenly believing that neurodivergent people are not competent enough to understand their own gender or sexuality.[8]

Another intersection between queer, trans, and neurodivergent people is that LGBTQIA people and neurodivergent people have had to fight against the pathologization of their bodyminds. Queer and trans people have battled medical and psychiatric misunderstandings of their sexualities and gender identities as pathological and in need of a cure, fought the legal system in its attempt to curtail them living out their gendered and sexual lives, and struggled against the ecclesial structures that have portrayed their embodiments as sinful and in need of healing.

Similarly, neurodivergent people have fought pathologizing ways of understanding bodyminds that differ from the neuromajority, creating the "neurodiversity paradigm" to counter the pathologization of the medical paradigm. This paradigm holds that "neurodiversity is a natural and valuable form of human diversity" and that there is no one normal or healthy type of bodymind, though power inequalities exist between neurotypical and neurodivergent people, just as they do in other forms of diversity (gender, sexuality, race, culture, etc.).[9]

It is vital for everyone serving in ministry with LGBTQIA and neurodivergent youth to work from a neurodiversity paradigm rather than a pathology paradigm. This commitment honors the embodiment of neurodivergent youth as sacred and revelatory of the image of God and a gift to the communities to which they belong. Additionally, working from a neurodiversity paradigm means honoring the wisdom and knowledge of neurodivergent youth. They are the experts on their own lives and experiences.

Both neurodivergent and LGBTQIA people have had "expert" knowledge imposed on them in ways that have promoted misunderstanding and enacted harm. Learn about neurodivergent people from the voices of neurodivergent people. As Finn V. Gratton, a queer, autistic, nonbinary, transgender psychotherapist, helpfully states, when our "assumptions are created by media sensationalism, by incomplete or biased research, or by ingroup privileged status that is not cognizant of the experience of outside group members, we miss what we need to see in order to be welcoming and supportive care providers."[10]

Finally, our political moment has ushered in renewed and particularly malicious forms of stigmatization for both queer and trans people *and* for neurodivergent people. The current presidential administration is rapidly defunding autism research, the U.S. Secretary of Health and Human Services regularly promulgates unscientific theories about the cause of autism, and many measures aimed to help neurodivergent people live well in our society are being cancelled in the administration's erasure of DEI initiatives.

A statement from the Autistic Self Advocacy Network points to the dire consequences of misinformation, saying, "When top officials spread misinformation about autism, autistic people suffer. . . . This fear and stigma makes it harder for autistic people to find inclusion and acceptance in school, in the workplace, and in our communities. It leads frightened families to pursue fraudulent 'cures'. . . that actually do risk unnecessary injury and death."[11] Both LGBTQIA and neurodivergent youth need the allyship of individuals and communities of faith who will stand with them in striving for a society of inclusion and justice that honors the embodiment of human difference.

CONSIDERATIONS FOR CULTIVATING NEUROINCLUSIVITY

Gratton says, "For many transgender and autistic people to be acceptable, they have to *not* be themselves, which runs perilously close to not being."[12] This is true not only for trans and autistic people but also for many LGBTQIA and neurodivergent people who are constantly asked to fit their bodyminds into heteronormative, gender binary, and neuromajority designed communities. Just as LGBTQIA youth have a finely tuned radar that seeks out signs of a community's commitment to queer and trans welcome and belonging, neurodivergent youth know when their bodyminds have been considered in how a community is formed.

For example, many neurodivergent youth experience sound sensitivity that can be accommodated with quieter music, making noise-reducing headphones available, or even a quiet room that a youth can retreat to for a time when the larger youth space is too auditorily overwhelming. Others experience light sensitivity that can make bright, fluorescent-lit rooms hard to be in for long periods.

In high-touch communities where hugs and handshakes are the norm, neurodivergent youth with touch sensitivity may appreciate having their desire for less touch or no touch respected. Often in crowded spaces where bodies are in close proximity–which describe many youth events– having some seating that is spaced out a bit for those who don't want to be right next to others can help some neurodivergent youth feel more included, as can having some open spaces for people to move their bodies while participating in the worship service, Bible study, or other activity.

Many neuro-informed congregations also have a sensory library filled with objects that can help neurodivergent people better participate in the community. These libraries often include finger labyrinths, thera-putty, and fidget toys that help many neurodivergent people to focus better and regulate their bodyminds; ear plugs to reduce the volume of sound in loud rooms; rocking chairs that allow for self-stimulating (stimming) by moving the body; weighted blankets or lap pads; and a host of other objects.[13]

Lund says, "Inclusion in society and in the church means people with Autism, dementia, anxiety, ADHD, PTSD, and other brain differences are not an afterthought but part of the intentional design of what it means to be included in community."[14] Whether you're at the outset of learning what it means in practice to cultivate LGBTQIA-inclusive community or you've been at it for many years, I hope that you will consider building into that commitment a practical orientation toward neuroinclusivity as well. Our experience of a community's richness and our ability to witness the working of the Divine in the world increases when a wider diversity of people can feel at home in an inclusive place of belonging that has our bodyminds in mind.

KEEP GOING!

This chapter is a true *brief* introduction! There's so much more to learn and know in cultivating a neuroinclusive ministry for youth and for all ages. Continue learning from the wisdom of neurodivergent people who put their knowledge and experience into books, blogs, podcasts, and videos to help you become neuro-informed. Listen to neurodivergent youth who tell you what they need to experience a deeper sense of belonging.

One book that would be helpful to read as a follow-up to this chapter is *Blessed Minds: Breaking the Silence about Neurodiversity,* by Sarah Griffith Lund. Additionally, youth ministry leaders can enroll in the Neurodiversity and Youth Ministry online module called "Cultivating God's Brainforest" through Princeton Seminary's Institute for Youth Ministry.[15] Finally, for neurodivergent queer youth in your ministry who may desire further resources for reflecting on their own queer or trans neurodivergent bodyminds, consider having available a copy of the book *Queerly Autistic*, by queer, autistic author Erin Ekins, written specifically for youth.[16] In the notes for this chapter, you can find other book resources, and in the appendix at the end of the book, I provide more web and community resources.

There has never been a time when adult allies are as vital as they are right now, both for queer and trans youth and for neurodivergent youth. Your faith community may very well be the one place where LGBTQIA and neurodivergent youth in your city or town know they can bring the fullness of their bodyminds into relational space where they will be known and loved and honored for the divine beauty of their trans, queer, and neuroqueer selves. That will be a gift to them, just as they will be a gift to your faith community.[17]

Appendix

National and Local Resources for Supporting LGBTQIA Youth

This appendix is a worksheet that you should fill out and keep on hand in cases when an LGBTQIA youth is in need of immediate support in some area of his, her, or their life. Make copies of this worksheet for other ministry leaders in your congregation or organization.

SUICIDE PREVENTION RESOURCES

988 Suicide & Crisis Lifeline

Website: www.988lifeline.org
Phone: 988
Description: Easy to remember in times of distress, 988 is a nationwide 24/7 suicide prevention lifeline. Note that this is not an LGBTQIA-specific resource and that, in response to federal budget cuts and anti-DEI mandates in 2025, it has stopped offering specialized services for LGBTQIA youth.

Suicide Prevention Resource Center

Website: www.sprc.org
Phone: 988
Description: SPRC provides resources for training and prevention on their website. You can access a suicide prevention state coordinator who can help with training for suicide prevention in your state by visiting the "states" section of the website at www.sprc.org/states.

Faith. Hope. Life. (Part of the National Action Alliance for Suicide Prevention)

Website: www.theactionalliance.org/faith-hope-life
Description: Offers resources for faith communities to engage in suicide prevention, drawing on the strengths of varied faith traditions that promote life and prevent suicide.

The Trevor Project (LGBTQ+ Suicide Prevention)

Website: www.thetrevorproject.org
Phone: 1-866-488-7386 (This is a 24/7 suicide prevention lifeline.)
Description: The Trevor Project is the leading national organization providing suicide prevention to LGBTQ+ youth and young adults (ages 18–24). They operate a 24/7 phone line, text line, and chat service and have resources on their website for youth and for professionals involved in suicide prevention.

Trans Lifeline (Trans-specific Suicide Prevention)

Website: www.translifeline.org
Phone: 877-565-8860 (U.S.) or 877-330-6366 (Canada)
Description: A hotline for trans people in crisis staffed entirely *by* trans people. See website for current hours.

Local Resources:

1. _____

Website: _____

Phone: _____

Description: _____

_____

_____

2. _____

Website: _____

Phone: _____

Description: _____

_____

_____

HOMELESSNESS RESOURCES AND LGBTQIA-FRIENDLY SHELTERS

True Colors United

Website: www.truecolorsunited.org
Description: True Colors United operates the National Youth Forum on Homelessness that engages in analysis and policy advocacy and all forum members have experienced homelessness themselves.

Ali Forney Center (New York City)

Website: www.aliforneycenter.org
Description: Ali Forney is one of the largest LGBTQ+ youth shelters in the country and maintains a list of centers and shelters for LGBTQ+ homeless youth across the nation on their website.

Local Center/Shelter: _____

Phone: _____

Website: _____

Is this center/shelter (check one): ____ LGBTQIA-specific or ____ LGBTQIA-friendly

Date of visit or contact with shelter to learn about services: _____

Notes and description of services: _____

_____

_____

Local Center/Shelter: _____

Phone: _____

Website: _____

Is this center/shelter (check one): ____ LGBTQIA-specific or ____ LGBTQIA-friendly

Date of visit or contact with shelter to learn about services: _____

Notes and description of services: _____

_____

_____

THERAPISTS I TRUST TO SEE LGBTQIA YOUTH AND THEIR FAMILIES

1. _____

Phone: _____ *Email:* _____

Notes on my contact with them: _____

_____

_____

2. _____

Phone: _____ *Email:* _____

Notes on my contact with them: _____

_____

_____

3. _____

Phone: _____ *Email:* _____

Notes on my contact with them: _____

_____

_____

PARENTAL/FAMILY RESOURCES AND SUPPORT GROUPS

Family Acceptance Project

Website: https://familyproject.sfsu.edu

Description: The Family Acceptance Project is a resource for families and those working with the families of LGBTQ youth that can help address questions and concerns and increase acceptance among families for their LGBTQ children.

PFLAG

Website: www.pflag.org

Description: PFLAG is a network of over 360 chapters nationwide offering meetings for peer support and education to the family and friends of LGBTQ+ people.

Local chapter: _____

Meeting location: _____

Meeting time/date: _____

Local contact person: _____

Other Local Resources for Parents/Families: _____

_____

_____

_____

_____

LGBTQIA TEEN CENTERS AND SCHOOL RESOURCES

CenterLink: The Community of LGBTQ Centers

Website: www.lgbtcenters.org

Description: CenterLink is a directory of local LGBTQ centers; some are youth oriented and others are for youth and adults. This site will help you explore what LGBTQ centers exist in your geographic region.

Local LGBTQ Teen Center (or community center with teen services):

_____

Phone: _____

Website: _____

Is this center (check one): _____ Teen-specific or _____ Offers Teen Services

Date of visit or contact with center to learn about services: _____

Notes and description of services: _____

_____

_____

Local School: _____

Does the school have a Gay-Straight Alliance or similar organization: ___ Y ___ N

School Contact trusted to support LGBTQIA students: _____

Phone: _____ *Email:* _____

Local School: _____

Does the school have a Gay-Straight Alliance or similar organization: ___ Y ___ N

School contact trusted to support LGBTQIA students: _____

Phone: _____ *Email:* _____

Local School: _____

Does the school have a Gay-Straight Alliance or similar organization: ___ Y ___ N

School contact trusted to support LGBTQIA students: _____

Phone: _____ *Email:* _____

NEURODIVERSITY RESOURCES

Child Mind Institute

Website: childmind.org
Description: A nonprofit focused on children's mental health, including neurodiversity, with helpful informational resources for care and education.

Neuroqueer: The Writings of Dr. Nick Walker

Website: neuroqueer.com
Description: Dr. Nick Walker, a scholar and educator who has contributed to the neurdiversity paradigm and neuroqueer theory, has made available on this site many of his writings helpful for education on neurodivergence.

Galileo Church

Website: galileochurch.org

Description: Galileo church in Fort Worth, Texas, is a model congregation that pairs a commitment of justice for LGBTQ+ people with a commitment to welcome and inclusivity for people with mental illness and emotional distress, and it is a church that celebrates neurodiversity in its neuro-informed ministry.

The Theology & Neurodiversity Project

Website: theologyandneurodiversity.com

Description: A repository of resources, essays, and online courses to equip ministry leaders in neuroinclusive ministry and theology.

United Church of Christ Mental Health Network

Website: mhn-ucc.org

Description: The UCC denomination has developed a robust network of mental health ministry resources, including some addressing neurodiversity.

Notes

Preface to the Updated Edition

1. Ricardo Martinez, "Making Sense of the Trump Administration's Anti-LGBTQ+ Executive Orders," *GLAD LAW: GLBTQ Legal Advocates & Defenders*, February 4, 2025, https://www.gladlaw.org/making-sense-of-the-trump-administrations-anti-lgbtq-executive-orders/.

2. Donald Trump, "Protecting Children from Chemical and Surgical Mutilation," The White House, January 28, 2025, https://www.whitehouse.gov/presidential-actions/2025/01/protecting-children-from-chemical-and-surgical-mutilation/.

3. Donald Trump, "Ending Radical Indoctrination in K-12 Schooling," The White House, January 29, 2025, https://www.whitehouse.gov/presidential-actions/2025/01/ending-radical-indoctrination-in-k-12-schooling/.

4. ACLU, "Mapping Attacks on LGBTQ Rights in U.S. State Legislatures in 2025," American Civil Liberties Union, updated August 8, 2025, https://www.aclu.org/legislative-attacks-on-lgbtq-rights-2025.

5. ACLU, "Mapping Attacks on LGBTQ Rights in U.S. State Legislatures in 2024," American Civil Liberties Union, December 6, 2024, https://www.aclu.org/legislative-attacks-on-lgbtq-rights-2024.

6. ACLU, "Mapping Attacks on LGBTQ Rights in U.S. State Legislatures in 2023," American Civil Liberties Union, December 21, 2023, https://www.aclu.org/legislative-attacks-on-lgbtq-rights-2023.

7. The Trevor Project, "2024 U.S. National Survey on the Mental Health of LGBTQ+ Young People," The Trevor Project, accessed June 24, 2025, https://www.thetrevorproject.org/survey-2024/.

8. Trevor News, "The Trevor Project's Crisis Line Volume Continues to Increase Following Inauguration Day," The Trevor Project, January 22, 2025, https://www.thetrevorproject.org/blog/the-trevor-projects-crisis-line-volume-continues-to-increase-following-inauguration-day/#:~:text=This%20volume%20increase%20follows%20a,day%20after%20the%202024%20elections.

9. Maggie Astor, "Trump Administration Will End L.G.B.T.Q. Suicide Prevention Service," *New York Times*, June 18, 2025, https://www.nytimes.com/2025/06/18/well/lgbtq-988-suicide-prevention.html.

10. Taylor W. Burton Edwards, "What Is the Church's Position on Homosexuality?" The People of the United Methodist Church, accessed June 25, 2025, https://www.umc.org/en/content/ask-the-umc-what-is-the-churchs-position

-on-homosexuality?gad_source=1&gad_campaignid=22546684041&gbraid=0AA AAAD0t2uW9ul9Hmi0bM3YALOJ8sapfW&gclid=CjwKCAjwvO7CBhAqEiw A9q2YJQPFmaE_EpIIAU3n5Rrn_fj08IQFU4QiAa4gIcNXXyuHM0_g14Dcw RoCP70QAvD_BwE.

11. Reformed Church in America, "Statements of General Synod," Reformed Church in America, accessed June 25, 2025, https://www.rca.org/synod/statements/#sexuality.

12. Jeff Brumley, "AWAB and CBF's Affirming Network Merge," *Baptist News Global*, June 17, 2024, https://baptistnews.com/article/awab-and-cbfs-affirming-network-merge/.

13. For example, Arthur David Canales, *Pastoral Care to and Ministry with LGBTQ Youth and Young Adults* (Wipf & Stock, 2022); Leigh Finke, ed., *Queerfully and Wonderfully Made: A Guide for LGBTQ+ Christian Teens* (Beaming Books, 2020); Leigh Finke, ed., *Welcoming and Affirming: A Guide to Supporting and Working with LGBTQ+ Christian Youth* (Broadleaf Books, 2020); Ross Murray, *Made, Known, Loved: Developing LGBTQ-Inclusive Youth Ministry* (Fortress, 2021).

14. The Trevor Project, "The Trevor Project Research Brief: Accepting Adults Reduce Suicide Attempts among LGBTQ Youth," The Trevor Project, June 2019, https://www.thetrevorproject.org/wp-content/uploads/2019/06/Trevor-Project-Accepting-Adult-Research-Brief_June-2019.pdf.

Introduction and Terminology

1. One aspect of language that is particularly important is the use of "microaggressions." For more, see Cody J. Sanders and Angela Yarber, *Microaggressions in Ministry: Confronting the Hidden Violence of Everyday Church* (Westminster John Knox, 2015).

2. I am indebted to Avery Belyeu for articulating the importance of these questions. Email message to author, August 19, 2016. Used by permission.

Chapter 1: A Brief Guide to Gender Identity and Expression

1. Nicholas M. Teich, *Transgender 101: A Simple Guide to a Complex Issue* (Columbia University Press, 2012), 2, 15.

2. Jeffrey Fishberger, Phoenix Schneider, and Henry Ng, "Coming Out as You," The Trevor Project, accessed June 27, 2025, https://www.thetrevorproject.org/wp-content/uploads/2017/09/ComingOutAsYou.pdf. Also see The Trevor Project, "Resources about Gender Identity," The Trevor Project, accessed June 26, 2025, https://www.thetrevor project.org/resources/category/gender-identity/.

3. Three of the most helpful and accessible books addressing the theological and biblical questions pertaining to gender identity are Virginia Ramey Mollenkott, *Omnigender: A Trans-religious Approach*, rev. and exp. (Pilgrim, 2007); and Justin

Tanis, *Trans-Gendered: Theology, Ministry, and Communities of Faith* (Pilgrim, 2003); Austen Hartke, *Transforming: The Bible and the Lives of Transgender Christians*, updated and expanded (Westminster John Knox, 2023).

4. Anne Fausto-Sterling. *Sexing the Body: Gender Politics and the Construction of Sexuality* (Basic Books, 2000), cited in Myra J. Hird, "Queer(y)ing Intersex: Reflections on Counselling People with Intersex Conditions," in *Feeling Queer or Queer Feelings? Radical Approaches to Counselling Sex, Sexualities and Genders*, ed. Lyndsey Moon (Routledge, 2008), 54.

5. Hird, "Queer(y)ing Intersex," 60.

6. The Intersex Society of North America is a helpful resource for understanding the complexity of these differences that exist from birth for so many people and accessing statistics in more detail, online at: http://www.isna.org.

7. Tam Sanger, "Queer(y)ing Gender and Sexuality: Transpeople's Lived Experiences and Intimate Partnerships," in Moon, *Feeling Queer or Queer Feelings?*, 73.

8. One recent and highly accessible text introducing readers to this research is Teich, *Transgender 101*.

9. Hird, "Queer(y)ing Intersex," 60.

10. Hird, "Queer(y)ing Intersex," 67.

11. Teich, *Transgender 101*, 42 (italics in the original).

12. Carra Hughes Greer, email message to author, August 19, 2016. Used by permission.

13. Teich, *Transgender 101*, 115.

14. Tanis, *Trans-Gendered*, 56.

15. Genny Beemyn and Susan Rankin, *The Lives of Transgender People* (Columbia University Press, 2011), 40, 43.

16. Beemyn and Rankin, *The Lives of Transgender People*, 45.

17. Teich, *Transgender 101*, 43.

18. Tanis, *Trans-Gendered*, 147.

19. Beemyn and Rankin, *The Lives of Transgender People*, 44.

20. Tanis, *Trans-Gendered*, 149.

21. Tanis, *Trans-Gendered*, 149.

22. Tanis, *Trans-Gendered*, 153.

23. I am indebted to Avery Belyeu for raising the importance of this practice in a youth ministry setting. Email message to author, August 20, 2016.

24. Again, I am indebted to Ave ry Belyeu for bringing to my attention the harm of these gendered divisions to cisgender people, too. Email message to author, August 20, 2016.

25. Greer, email message to author, August 19, 2016. Used by permission.

Chapter 2: A Brief Guide to Sexual/Affectional Orientation

1. Kelly Brown Douglas, *Sexuality and the Black Church: A Womanist Perspective* (Orbis Books, 1999), 6.

2. Lisa M. Diamond, *Sexual Fluidity: Understanding Women's Love and Desire* (Harvard University Press, 2008), 127 (italics in the original).

3. Diamond, *Sexual Fluidity*, 94.

4. "About Asexuality," The Asexual Visibility & Education Network, accessed July 20, 2016, http://www.asexuality.org/?q=overview.html.

5. For a vast repository of information on asexuality, including first-person narratives, see The Asexual Visibility & Education Network, currently one of the best online archives of resources for understanding asexuality and connecting with the Ace Community; www.asexuality.org.

6. Paul Cox, "'We're Married, We Just Don't Have Sex'," *The Guardian*, September 7, 2008, accessed July 19, 2016, https://www.theguardian.com/lifeandstyle/2008/sep/08/relationships.healthandwellbeing.

7. Cox, "We're Married, We Just Don't Have Sex."

8. Darren Langdridge, "Are You Angry or Are You Heterosexual? A Queer Critique of Lesbian and Gay Models of Identity Development," in *Feeling Queer or Queer Feelings? Radical Approaches to Counselling Sex, Sexualities and Genders*, ed. Lyndsey Moon (Routledge, 2008), 28.

9. Langdridge, "Are You Angry or Are You Heterosexual?," 23.

10. I am indebted to Carra Hughes Greer for this insight and its importance in this discussion. Email message to author, August 19, 2016.

11. Diamond, *Sexual Fluidity*, 134.

12. Diamond, *Sexual Fluidity*, 3.

13. Diamond, *Sexual Fluidity*, 141 (italics added).

14. Tam Sanger, "Queer(y)ing Gender and Sexuality: Transpeople's Lived Experiences and Intimate Partnerships," in Moon, *Feeling Queer or Queer Feelings?*, 75.

15. Joretta L. Marshall, *Counseling Lesbian Partners* (Westminster John Knox, 1997), 17.

16. Patrick S. Cheng, *Rainbow Theology: Bridging Race, Sexuality, and Spirit* (Seabury Books, 2013), 89.

17. Cheng, *Rainbow Theology*, 90.

18. Cheng, *Rainbow Theology*, 101.

19. To develop an understanding of *machismo* in relation to LGBTQIA people, see Miguel A. De La Torre, "Confessions of a Latino Macho: From Gay Basher to Gay Ally," in *Out of the Shadows into the Light: Christianity and Homosexuality*, ed. Miguel A. De La Torre (Chalice, 2009).

20. For an overview of these statements, see "Health and Medical Organization Statements on Sexual Orientation, Gender Identity/Expression and 'Reparative Therapy,'" Lambda Legal, accessed September 21, 2025, https://legacy.lambdalegal.org/publications/health-and-med-orgs-stmts-on-sex-orientation-and-gender-identity.

21. Ian Lovett, "After 37 Years of Trying to Change People's Sexual Orientation, Group Is to Disband," *New York Times,* June 20, 2013, http://www.nytimes.com/2013/06/21/us/group-that-promoted-curing-gays-ceases-operations.html?_r=0.

22. James B. Nickoloff, "Sexuality: A Queer Omission in U.S. Latino/a Theology," *Journal of Hispanic/Latino Theology* 10, no. 3 (2003): 46.

23. Nickoloff, "Sexuality."

24. One very accessible text addressing the biblical texts presumed to speak about homosexuality is Matthew Vines, *God and the Gay Christian: The Biblical Case in Support of Same-Sex Relationships* (Convergent Books, 2014). Another brief book that I have often recommended to parents and family is Walter Wink, ed., *Homosexuality and Christian Faith: Questions of Conscience for the Churches* (Fortress, 1999).

Chapter 3: A Brief Guide to Ministry amid Questions and Crisis

1. Nicholas M. Teich, *Transgender 101: A Simple Guide to a Complex Issue* (Columbia University Press, 2012), 43–44.

2. Julie Tilsen, *Therapeutic Conversations with Queer Youth: Transcending Homonormativity and Constructing Preferred Identities* (Jason Aronson, 2013), 41–42.

3. Darnell L. Moore, "Coming Out or Inviting In?: Part I," *The Feminist Wire*, July 12, 2012, http://www.thefeministwire.com/2012/07/coming-out-or-inviting-in-reframing-disclosure-paradigms-part-i/.

4. Moore, "Coming Out or Inviting In?: Part I."

5. Darnell L. Moore, "Coming Out or Inviting In?: Part II," *The Feminist Wire*, July 13, 2012, http://www.thefeministwire.com/2012/07/coming-out-or-inviting-in-part-ii/.

6. Tilsen, *Therapeutic Conversations with Queer Youth*, 47 (italics in the original).

7. Joseph G. Kosciw, Caitlin M. Clark, and Leesh Menard, *The 2021 National School Climate Survey: The Experiences of LGBTQ+ Youth in Our Nation's Schools* (GLSEN, 2022), https://www.glsen.org/sites/default/files/2022-10/NSCS-2021-Full-Report.pdf.

8. Kosciw et al., *The 2021 National School Climate Survey*, xv.

9. Kosciw et al., *The 2021 National School Climate Survey*, xvi–xvii.

10. Genny Beemyn and Susan Rankin, *The Lives of Transgender People* (Columbia University Press, 2011), 96.

11. Beemyn and Rankin, *The Lives of Transgender People*, 97.

12. Beemyn and Rankin, *The Lives of Transgender People*, 83.

13. Iris Marion Young, *Justice and the Politics of Difference* (Princeton University Press, 1990), 61.

14. Kosciw et al., *The 2021 National School Climate Survey*, xx.

15. The Trevor Project, "Homelessness and Housing Instability among LGBTQ Youth," The Trevor Project, accessed July 3, 2025, https://www.thetrevorproject.org/wp-content/uploads/2022/02/Trevor-Project-Homelessness-Report.pdf.

16. The Trevor Project, "Homelessness and Housing Instability among LGBTQ Youth."

17. Lance Freeman and Darrick Hamilton, "A Count of Homeless Youth in New York City" (Empire State Coalition of Youth and Family Services, 2008).

18. The Ali Forney Center, http://www.aliforneycenter.org/.

19. "National Youth Forum on Homelessness," True Colors United, accessed July 3, 2025, https://truecolorsunited.org/our-work/youth-collaboration/national-youth-forum-on-homelessness/.

20. The 360 local chapters of PFLAG, an organization of parents and other allies of LGBTQ+ youth, can be found on their website: http://www.pflag.org.

21. U.S. Department of Health and Human Services (HHS), National Strategy for Suicide Prevention (HHS, 2024), 8.

22. Based on statistics from 2010. "Mental Health and Suicide Risk among High School Students and Protective Factors—Youth Risk Behavior Survey, United States, 2023," *Morbidity and Mortality Weekly Report*, October 10, 2024, https://www.cdc.gov/mmwr/volumes/73/su/su7304a9.htm.

23. Michael King et al., "A Systematic Review of Mental Disorder, Suicide, and Deliberate Self Harm in Lesbian, Gay and Bisexual People," *BCM Psychiatry* 8, no. 70 (2008): 1. See also Cody J. Sanders, *Christianity, LGBTQ Suicide, and the Souls of Queer Folk* (Lexington, 2020).

24. U.S. Department of Health and Human Services, National Strategy for Suicide Prevention, 8.

25. Jaime M. Grant, Lisa A. Mottet, and Justin Tanis, *Injustice at Every Turn: A Report of the National Transgender Discrimination Survey* (National Center for Transgender Equality and National Gay and Lesbian Task Force, 2011), 1.

26. Cody J. Sanders, "Re-Visioning the Care of Souls: The Praxis of Pastoral Care in the Context of LGBTQ Suicide" (PhD diss., Brite Divinity School, 2015), 111.

27. Sanders, "Re-Visioning the Care of Souls," 114.

28. Sanders, "Re-Visioning the Care of Souls," 97.

29. Shawn Christopher Shea, *The Practical Art of Suicide Assessment: A Guide for Mental Health Professionals and Substance Abuse Counselors* (Wiley, 2002), 101–3.

30. Carra Hughes Greer, email message to author, August 20, 2016. Used by permission.

31. See http://www.thetrevorproject.org.

32. See http://www.translifeline.org.

33. I am indebted to Avery Belyeu for the resourceful idea of creating a worksheet of national and local resources. Email message to author, August 21, 2016.

34. I am indebted to Carra Hughes Greer for this suggestion. Email message to author, August 20, 2016.

35. See "States and Territories," Suicide Prevention Resource Center, accessed August 23, 2016, http://www.sprc.org/states.

36. Greer, email message to author, August 20, 2016. Used by permission.

37. Wayne E. Oates, *The Christian Pastor*, 3rd ed. rev. (Westminster John Knox, 1982), 263–83.

Chapter 4: A Brief Guide to Ministry with Parents and Families

1. "Family Acceptance Project," San Francisco State University, accessed July 28, 2016, https://familyproject.sfsu.edu.

2. Substance Abuse and Mental Health Services Administration (SAMHSA), *A Practitioner's Resource Guide: Helping Families to Support Their LGBT Children*, HHS Publication no. PEP14-LGBTKIDS (Substance Abuse and Mental Health Services Administration, 2014), 3. Also available online at https://familyproject.sfsu.edu/sites/default/files/documents/FamilySupportForLGBTChildrenGuidance.pdf.

3. SAMHSA, *A Practitioner's Resource Guide*.

4. Julie Tilsen, *Therapeutic Conversations with Queer Youth: Transcending Homonormativity and Constructing Preferred Identities* (Jason Aronson, 2013), 47 (italics in the original).

5. Tilsen, *Therapeutic Conversations with Queer Youth*, 44.

6. Nicholas M. Teich, *Transgender 101: A Simple Guide to a Complex Issue* (Columbia University Press, 2012), 35.

7. SAMHSA, *A Practitioner's Resource Guide*, 9.

8. Catlin Ryan et al., "Family Rejection as a Predictor of Negative Health Outcomes in White and Latino Lesbian, Gay and Bisexual Young Adults," *Pediatrics* 123, no. 1 (2009): 346.

9. SAMHSA, *A Practitioner's Resource Guide*, 2.

10. I treat the varied ways that "love" has been practiced toward LGBTQIA people in a previous publication: Cody J. Sanders, *Queer Lessons for Churches on the Straight and Narrow: What All Christians Can Learn from LGBTQ Lives* (Faithlab, 2013).

11. Carra Hughes Greer, email message to author, August 20, 2016. Used by permission.

12. Caitlin Ryan and Stuart Chen-Hayes. "Educating and Empowering Families of LGBTQ K-12 Students" in Emily S. Fisher and Karen Komosa-Hawkins, eds., *Creating Safe and Supportive Learning Environments: A Guide for Working with Lesbian, Gay, Bisexual, Transgender, and Questioning Youth and Families* (Routledge, 2013), 209–27.

13. See "Therapists," *Psychology Today*, accessed August 3, 2016, https://therapists.psychologytoday.com/rms/.

14. SAMHSA, *A Practitioner's Resource Guide*, 8.

15. Caitlin Ryan and Donna Futterman, *Lesbian & Gay Youth: Care & Counseling* (Columbia University Press, 1998), 68.

16. Teich, *Transgender 101*, 32.

17. Teich, *Transgender 101*, 32.

18. Ryan and Futterman, *Lesbian & Gay Youth*, 69.

19. SAMHSA, *A Practitioner's Resource Guide*, 11.

20. SAMHSA, *A Practitioner's Resource Guide*, 9.

21. For further discussion on the use of narrative and story in pastoral care, see Suzanne M. Coyle, *Uncovering Spiritual Narratives: Using Story in Pastoral Care and Ministry* (Fortress, 2014).

22. Children's Bureau, "Clergy as Mandatory Reporters of Child Abuse and Neglect," accessed July 12, 2025, https://cwig-prod-prod-drupal-s3fs-us-east-1.s3.amazonaws.com/public/documents/clergy-mandated-reporters.pdf?VersionId=Z_dIjzYYgtEWVGrwBKy1V83e.b.Y0YIE.

23. See PFLAG, accessed July 28, 2016, https://www.pflag.org.

24. Ryan and Futterman, *Lesbian & Gay Youth*, 70–71.

25. Tilsen, *Therapeutic Conversations with Queer Youth*, 98.

26. Avery Belyeu, email message to author, August 21, 2016. Used by permission.

27. Belyeu, email message to author, August 21, 2016.

28. Belyeu, email message to author, August 21, 2016.

29. SAMHSA, *A Practitioner's Resource Guide*, 11.

30. I am indebted to Davi Reese Weasley for the encouragement to think about spiritual practices, like prayer, which can be helpful in the lives of parents and families.

Chapter 5: A Brief Guide to Pastoral and Mentoring Relationships with LGBTQIA Youth

1. Carrie Doehring, *The Practice of Pastoral Care: A Postmodern Approach*, Revised and Expanded (Westminster John Knox, 2015), xv.

2. Julie Tilsen, *Therapeutic Conversations with Queer Youth: Transcending Homonormativity and Constructing Preferred Identities* (Jason Aronson, 2013), 72.

3. For more information on such laws, see "Laws That Prohibit the 'Promotion of Homosexuality,'" GLSEN, accessed July 14, 2025, https://www.glsen.org/research/laws-prohibit-promotion-homosexuality-impacts-and-implicatio.

4. See www.siecus.org.

5. See www.advocatesforyouth.org.

6. Sue Hyde, *Come Out and Win: Organizing Yourself, Your Community, and Your World* (Beacon, 2007), 153–4.

7. Doehring, *The Practice of Pastoral Care*, 5.

8. James B. Nelson, *Body Theology* (Westminster/John Knox, 1992), 50.

9. James B. Nickoloff, "Sexuality: A Queer Omission in U.S. Latino/a Theology," *Journal of Hispanic/Latino Theology* 10, no. 3 (2003): 50.

10. Nelson, *Body Theology*, 50.

11. Tilsen, *Therapeutic Conversations with Queer Youth*, 6 (italics in the original).

12. Nickoloff, "Sexuality," 42.

13. Judith Butler, *Notes toward a Performative Theory of Assembly* (Harvard University Press, 2015), 40.

Chapter 6: A Brief Guide to Queer Neurodiversity

1. *Neurospicy* is a slang term used by some, but not all, neurodivergent people to describe many and varied ways that bodyminds operate beyond neurotypical assumptions.

2. Sarah Griffith Lund, *Blessed Minds: Breaking the Silence about Neurodiversity* (Chalice, 2025), 17.

3. Nick Walker, *Neuroqueer Heresies: Notes on the Neurodiversity Paradigm, Autistic Empowerment, and Postnormal Possibilities* (Autonomous Press, 2021), 58.

4. Walker, *Neuroqueer Heresies*, 63. I highly encourage readers to access Walker's online article "Neurodiversity: Some Basic Terms & Definitions," *Neuroqueer: The Writings of Dr. Nick Walker*, accessed July 17, 2025, https://neuroqueer.com/neurodiversity-terms-and-definitions/.

5. Elizabeth Weir et al., "The Sexual Health, Orientation, and Activity of Autistic Adolescents and Adults," *Autism Research* 14, no. 11 (2021): 2342–54.

6. For a helpful summary of recent research, see "Autistic Individuals Are More Likely to Be LGBTQ+," University of Cambridge, accessed July 17, 2025, https://www.cam.ac.uk/research/news/autistic-individuals-are-more-likely-to-be-lgbtq.

7. Varun Warrier et al., "Elevated Rates of Autism, Other Neurodevelopmental and Psychiatric Diagnoses, and Autistic Traits in Transgender and Gender-Diverse Individuals," *Nature Communications* 11, no. 1 (2022).

8. John Anderson, "LGBTQIA+ and Neurodiversity: The Links between Neurodivergence and Being LGBTQ+," The Brain Charity, December 23, 2022, https://www.thebraincharity.org.uk/lgbtqia-neurodiversity-neurodivergent-lgbtq/.

9. Walker, *Neuroqueer Heresies*, 36.

10. Finn V. Gratton, *Supporting Transgender Autistic Youth and Adults: A Guide for Professionals and Families* (Jessica Kingsley Publishers, 2019), 20.

11. "Trump and Kennedy Spouting Dangerous Autism Misinformation," Autism Self Advocacy Network, April 10, 2025, https://autisticadvocacy.org/2025/04/trump-and-kennedy-spouting-dangerous-autism-misinformation/.

12. Gratton, *Supporting Transgender Autistic Youth and Adults*, 107.

13. You can find a wide variety of sensory toys and tools for a range of ages from National Autism Resources, https://nationalautismresources.com/sensory-toys/.

14. Lund, *Blessed Minds*, 36. Lund describes the ministry of several neuroinclusive congregations, including First Congregational Church of Greenwich, Connecticut, and Galileo Church in Fort Worth, Texas.

15. "Cultivating God's Brainforest," Institute for Youth Ministry, Princeton Theological Seminary, accessed July 17, 2025, https://iym.ptsem.edu/programs/cultivating-gods-brainforest/.

16. Erin Ekins, *Queerly Autistic: The Ultimate Guide for LGBTQIA+ Teens on the Spectrum* (Jessica Kingsley Publishers, 2021).

17. I am grateful to Luke Bitzkie for reading and providing feedback on this chapter.